GEORGE ORWELL

GEORGE ORWELL
THE POLITICAL PEN

KEITH FERRELL

M. Evans and Company, Inc.
New York

Selections from the following works have been reprinted with the permission of Harcourt Brace Jovanovich, Inc.:

Excerpt from *Animal Farm* by George Orwell, copyright 1946 by Harcourt Brace Jovanovich, Inc.; renewed 1974 by Sonia Orwell. Excerpts from *Burmese Days*, copyright 1934 by George Orwell; renewed 1962 by Sonia Pitt-Rivers. Excerpt from "The Spike" in *The Collected Essays, Journalism and Letters of George Orwell*, Volume 1, copyright © 1968 by Sonia Brownell Orwell. Excerpt from "The Lion and the Unicorn" in *The Collected Essays, Journalism and Letters of George Orwell*, Volume 2, copyright © 1968 by Sonia Brownell Orwell. Excerpt from "As I Please" in *The Collected Essays, Journalism and Letters of George Orwell*, Volume 3, copyright © 1968 by Sonia Brownell Orwell. Excerpt from *Homage to Catalonia* by George Orwell, copyright 1952, 1980 by Sonia Brownell Orwell. Excerpt from *Keep the Aspidistra Flying* by George Orwell. Excerpts from *Nineteen Eighty-Four* by George Orwell, copyright 1949 by Harcourt Brace Jovanovich, Inc.; renewed 1977 by Sonia Brownell Orwell. Excerpt from *The Road to Wigan Pier* by George Orwell. Excerpts from "A Hanging" and "Shooting an Elephant" in *Shooting an Elephant and Other Essays* by George Orwell, copyright 1950 by Sonia Brownell Orwell; renewed 1978 by Sonia Pitt-Rivers.

Library of Congress Cataloging in Publication Data

Ferrell, Keith.
 George Orwell, the political pen.

 Includes index.
 Summary: Examines the life of Eric Blair, the English writer who gained fame under the pen name George Orwell, and discusses his political philosophy as disclosed in his work.
 1. Orwell, George, 1903–1950—Biography—Juvenile literature. 2. Authors, English—20th century—Biography—Juvenile literature. 3. Politics in literature—Juvenile literature. [1. Orwell, George, 1903–1950. 2. Authors, English] I. Title.
PR6029.R8Z634 1985 828'.91209 [B] [92] 84-25932

ISBN 0-87131-444-4

M. Evans and Company, Inc.
216 East 49 Street
New York, New York 10017

Design by Diane Gedymin

Manufactured in the United States of America

9 8 7 6 5 4 3 2 1

FOR MY MOTHER,
ELIZABETH BOWMAN FERRELL,
WHOSE OPINIONS I RESPECT

CONTENTS

ONE: Indian Birth, British Boyhood 9
TWO: St. Cyprian's 23
THREE: Eric at Eton 45
FOUR: Blair in Burma 62
FIVE: Down, Out, and On the Way Up 77
SIX: *Orwell* 97
SEVEN: The Road to Disillusionment 113
EIGHT: Broadcasting Through the Blitz 133
NINE: Nineteen Forty-Eight 151
EPILOGUE: *Nineteen Eighty-Four* in 1984 (and Beyond) 159
Acknowledgments and References 171
The Works of George Orwell 174
Index 177

ONE

INDIAN BIRTH, BRITISH BOYHOOD

ALTHOUGH ERIC ARTHUR BLAIR would earn his fame under the name George Orwell, the family name was illustrious enough in its own right. Blairs had done things, they had gone places, they had made their mark. By the time Eric Blair was born in 1903, however, it was clear to all that the marks made were less bold with each generation, and the family's fortunes were not on the rise.

The peak of the Blairs' prestige had come four generations earlier, when Eric's great-great-grandfather, Charles Blair, owned Jamaican estates and plantations. (He also owned a large number of slaves.) Charles Blair died in 1802, and the inheritance he left Eric's great-grandfather, Charles Blair, Jr., was a large one; he was able to support his family comfortably. Thomas Richard Arthur Blair, Eric's grandfather, was born in 1802, the second son in the family, and the prospects he faced were less grand.

Primogeniture: This was the ancient word and the rule by which in the stratified British class system of the early nineteenth century, the right of inheritance belonged exclusively to the eldest son. Younger sons must face the world on their own, meet its challenges with their own personal resources. All they received from their family was their name. Still, Blair was a good, well-connected name, and a young man in Thomas Richard Arthur Blair's position found himself with several appealing options.

There was the army, into which a young man of good family could enter as a second lieutenant, and expect to rise swiftly to an even higher rank. Or there was the life of a colonial officer, serving the crown in one of the outposts of the empire, handling bureaucratic and managerial details. A third choice was the Church of England, then as much a social as religious focus for society. Churchmen had prestige of their own, and the communities they served revolved around them. Failing to achieve a career in the church or in the military or colonial service, a second son might find himself sinking into one of the professions (law or medicine) which at that time carried little honor and less income.

After a protracted period of travel and service in various minor colonial positions, Eric Blair's grandfather chose the church. Thomas Blair found himself, at twenty-seven, in Calcutta, being ordained an Anglican deacon, studying for the priesthood. His travels continued, he revealed a talent for the clergy, and he rose in the ranks of the church. In 1843 he was serving in Tasmania, and the bishop there made him a full member of the clergy. There was little doubt in his mind that when his travels ended and he returned to Britain a vicarage would be found for him, and he would settle into the not uncomfortable life of vicar.

Such a life had its own rules of propriety. Vicars were expected to be married, to raise families, and Thomas Blair had in fact become engaged to a well-born young woman during a stop in Cape Town, South Africa while traveling from India to Britain. It was Thomas Blair's plan to marry Emily Hare when he stopped in Cape Town en route back to India. But when he returned to Africa he discovered that the impatient Ms. Hare had broken the engagement during his absence and had already married another man. Thomas Blair was a practical man, a man of action as well as a man of God, and finding Emily unavailable he proceeded to marry her fifteen-year-old younger sister Frances, an attractive young woman whom everyone called Fanny.

In 1854 Thomas and Fanny Blair returned to Britain for good, ready to take up the life of vicar and vicar's wife in a pleasant parish. The Blair name and family connections served Thomas Blair well. Through the intercession of a relative of his mother's, he was made vicar of Milborne St. Andrew, in Dorset, a parish nearly a thousand years old. Founded in 1067, a century and a half before the signing of the Magna Charta, Milborne St. Andrew's church served the village of Milborne, and its vicar was also responsible for services and church duties in nearby Dewlish. The vicarage brought with it an income of nearly a thousand pounds. Ironically, that income was substantially larger than that received by Thomas Blair's older brother, Eric. Primogeniture sometimes took strange turns.

The country life in Dorset agreed with Thomas and Fanny Blair. They settled into their vicarage and produced eight children. Fanny would bear two more sons. On January 7, 1857 she gave birth to Richard Walmsley Blair, Eric Blair's father.

Richard Blair was ten years old when his father died. As the boy passed through his adolescence and approached the age when he must enter the world of adults, he, too, discovered the problems faced by a younger son. In addition, he was the youngest son of a family whose name was still respectable, but whose connections with more influential families had grown increasingly tenuous as time passed and memories of the vicar grew dim. Faced with the same choice as his father nearly four decades earlier—church, military, or colonial service—Richard Blair decided on the colonial service. He was eighteen years old on August 4, 1875, when he was accepted by the British government of India's Opium Department and given the rank of Assistant Sub-Deputy Opium Agent, fifth grade. It was an inauspicious beginning for a bureaucratic career in a government department whose existence grew more controversial each year.

The narcotic properties of opium had been known to medicine since the time of Galen, the Greek physician and scientist of the second century A.D. The commercial properties of this derivative of the poppy, and especially the Chinese market for opium as a medicine, had been exploited by Arab traders since the sixth century. Opium's virtues as a vice were introduced by European traders, Spanish and Dutch, and by 1729 the Chinese emperor was forced to try to control an increasingly serious problem. Opium "dens" where the drug was smoked were undermining the moral fiber of a generation of Chinese, and the emperor promised swift punishment by slow strangulation for operators of opium shops. The regulations did little to stop the traffic in opium, but until the arrival of the British the trade remained a largely unorganized affair.

The East India Company, cornerstone of the British Empire, found the opium industry in great disarray early in the eighteenth century. Sensing the profit to be taken from trade with the Chinese, whose market for opium continued to grow despite all prohibitions, the East India Company studied the harvest of poppies and manufacture of opium in Bengal, a large region in northeastern India, and examined a variety of means for controlling the opium trade with China. By 1773 the studies were complete. The opium industry was made a monopoly of the government of Bengal, while the industry itself was under the control of the East India Company. In Britain the drug remained illegal, although quantities of it were smuggled in and opium dens sprang up clandestinely in the larger cities.

For seventy-five years the trade grew; despite the vehement opposition of the Chinese government, whose laws proved powerless against the traders, despite growing uncertainty in Britain concerning the morality of the trade, and despite conflict which grew violent. (Although the so-called Opium War of 1839–1842 was sparked by a Chinese customs official's burning of a shipment of opium, the conflict sprang from more than simply the opium trade. The British were looking for an excuse

12

to end Chinese trade restrictions in general.) British military might subjugated the Chinese, treaties were drawn up establishing British ports in China, and although opium remained illegal and trade in the substance was still forbidden, the trade flourished.

By the 1850s traffic in opium was measured in thousands of chests of the drug, manufactured, transported, and sold each year, with each chest containing 160 pounds of Bengal opium. At its peak the opium trade with China was responsible for one-seventh of all revenues derived by the British Empire from operations in India. In 1858 the Chinese became aware that they would never stem the flow of opium. They decided instead to impose a tariff on opium imports. That course of action offered sufficient legal respectability for the British to proceed with legalizing the drug traffic and making opium a government monopoly and concern, rather than a business handled by a private company. This shift was marked by the Act for the Better Government of India, passed in 1858.

Concurrently, antiopium sentiment was building in Britain, much of it coming from the religious establishment. Exposés were written about British opium dens. There was little the opponents of the trade could do, however, other than file protests and make speeches proclaiming their moral indignation. The government took firm hold over the machinery of the opium trade, and retained much of its architecture, its ranks and positions. One of the positions was that of subdeputy opium agent, a position created in 1836 by the East India Company. Subdeputy agents were the men in charge of the actual production of the opium itself. This was the job and the responsibility to which eighteen-year-old Richard Blair found himself assigned.

It was a life of travel; few of Blair's postings lasted more than a few months. As a fifth-grade subdeputy he was moved at the whim of his superiors, filling a need here, taking over a vacancy there. During a period of famine he was made a relief officer in charge of operations at Bellary in south-central India.

Other posts at which he learned the particulars and peculiarities of opium production included Allahabad, Fuzabad, Shahjahanpur, and Tehta.

No matter how controversial the Opium Department might be in Britain, its officers in India could enjoy a comfortable life. Their salaries would never make them wealthy, but money went farther in India than in Britain. Even low-grade officers such as Richard Blair could afford spacious and well-furnished quarters with a staff of servants. The work that occupied Blair and other officers was mainly administrative. It was hard work but not unpleasant. For off-duty hours, every corner of the empire held a club to which the officers retired. Within the convivial and civilized confines of these clubs, young officers such as Blair could talk with other officers over drinks that were frequently raised in toasts to Queen Victoria, whose portraits were so prominently hung.

Blair enjoyed the prestige accorded him as a white, British officer in India, and in 1896 he met and married a young woman with whom he would, after a fashion, share that life. Blair was thirty-nine at the time and was stationed in Tehta, in the Indian province of Bihar in northeast India, near Nepal. The woman Blair married, Ida Limouzin, was twenty-one years old, of French and English ancestry, born into a family of merchants who had been established in Burma since early in the nineteenth century. Ida was a robust and cheerful young woman who enjoyed reading and possessed many strong opinions to which she gave frequent voice. But she also took pleasure in the domestic duties of running a house, and despite the difference in age between Ida and her husband, the marriage was a happy one from the start.

Tehta was one of the longer postings of Richard Blair's career, and he and Ida were still there in 1898 when their first child, Marjorie, was born. Early in 1903 Blair received orders transferring him to the city of Motihari in Bengal. The trip was planned with care, for Ida was pregnant again. They arrived in

Motihari without incident, and their second child was born there on June 25, 1903. The Blairs named their son Eric Arthur Blair. Before the boy was a year old plans were made for Ida and the children to return to Britain.

The decision to leave India was virtually expected of British officers' wives as their children grew older and approached school age. Typically, Ida Limouzin Blair applied herself to the details of the move with great energy and efficiency, carrying Eric in her arms and shepherding Marjorie up the gangplank onto the ship that would bear them home. She found a house in Henley-on-Thames, west of London, that they rented for nearly a year before moving to a slightly larger and more comfortable one. Neither house, though, measured up to the quarters they'd enjoyed in India, and certainly there was no room in Ida's budget for a staff of servants. But she did not complain. A good cook, she transformed inexpensive ingredients into delicious meals. Possessed of a strong, lively sense of humor, she made friends easily and soon became an important part of her community, with a large circle of friends. Her children were always clean and neatly dressed, and when they fell ill she tended them closely until their health was regained.

Young Eric was more sickly than Marjorie had been. The boy began experiencing bronchial difficulty before he was two, spending whole months indoors under the care of his mother, enduring frequent visits by the doctor. His illnesses and recuperations seemed to develop a pattern, with Eric growing increasingly active as he recovered, climbing through windows as though to escape from the house, splashing in puddles, laughing on visits to the sea, but too soon collapsing back into bed as his lungs grew heavy with fluid and his body was shaken by spells of heavy coughing. The child tolerated his illnesses as well as any child could, but Ida was not really surprised when one of Eric's first words was *beastly*. It was an apt and terse summation of his health, of the dreary English winter weather, and of the confinement his poor constitution imposed upon Eric and Ida.

Spring approached at last, though, and Eric began to gain strength and weight. As the weather improved, Ida sought to distract Eric and Marjorie with picnics on pretty afternoons. In the late summer there were expeditions to gather berries for pies, long walks on sunny days. When Ida was busy she hired young local women to walk with her children. Eric enjoyed being outdoors, and delighted in wandering along the banks of the river to watch fishermen work their lines, and displayed great curiosity about the names of plants and animals. His fascination with both domestic and farm animals resulted in the Blairs acquiring a menagerie of dogs, cats, guinea pigs, even rabbits. As Eric grew more sturdy he spent most of his time with his pets.

In the summer of 1907, Eric turned four. His birthday celebration was overshadowed later that summer by the return of his father from India. Richard Blair's stay in Henley was temporary—he was on a three-month leave from the Opium Department. He was pleased with the comfortable and well-run home that Ida had established in Henley and had named "Nutshell." Blair was equally pleased with his children's development. Marjorie was now nine years old, a self-possessed and cheerful schoolgirl who loved to read. Eric, whom Blair had not seen since the boy's infancy, was rosy cheeked and chubby, proud of his pets, surprisingly articulate for such a young boy.

It was a happy family, and one which would soon grow larger. Richard Blair, now fifty years old, a subdeputy opium agent, first grade, and his wife Ida, conceived another child during his leave. When Blair departed it was with the knowledge that his family was secure, and that this next tour of duty in India would be his last. Before too many more years passed, Blair would be able to retire and return home, with a service pension for the support of his household.

Once her husband had left for India, Ida set to work preparing Eric for school. She understood the importance of education in establishing a young man's prospects, and she had seen to it that Eric's educational preparations began early. During the winter months when Eric was often bedridden, Ida had introduced the boy to the wonderful distractions offered by the world of books. She sat for hours beside him, reading aloud children's stories, poetry, and letters from Richard Blair. Eric enjoyed the children's stories, particularly Beatrix Potter's tales of animals, but he was especially taken with poetry. Before he was five years old he had composed a poem of his own, a bit of exotic verse about a ferocious tiger with "chair-like teeth." The clever phrase reinforced Ida's opinion that Eric was a bright boy with precocious verbal skills. Throughout the spring of 1908, as she waited for her third child to be born, Ida gave thought to the selection of a good school for Eric.

The new baby arrived on April 6, 1908, and Ida named the girl after the month, with a nod toward her own French ancestry: *Avril* Blair. Eric and Marjorie were fascinated by the tiny girl and sat beside the crib for hours, watching her.

Not long after Avril's birth, Ida enrolled Eric in Sunnylands, a school operated by the local Anglican convent. For all her study of advertisements for other schools, Ida had finally selected one with which she was already familiar, Marjorie having entered Sunnylands when she reached school age. Ida was pleased not only with the solid educational foundation the nuns offered, but also with the school's reasonable tuition schedule. The Blairs, thanks to Richard's slow but steady rise through the ranks of the Opium Department, were well established in the upper range of the economic lower middle class, but tuition was still a factor in the choice of a school. The proximity of Sunnylands permitted Eric and Marjorie to attend classes as local students living at home, saving Ida the not inconsiderable room and board charges she would have faced had she chosen a school outside of Henley.

Sunnylands was a delight for Eric. The nuns who taught him were friendly and attentive, and in their classrooms the boy's brightness blossomed. He quickly learned to read, and his skills with words grew stronger daily. Eric passed effortlessly from primers and Beatrix Potter to more challenging books. Marjorie, another lover of books and reading, enjoyed sharing with her younger brother the books she had enjoyed, and by the time Eric was eight he had read *Tom Sawyer* by Mark Twain, some of Kipling's stories, a bit of Dickens, as well as a great variety of adventure stories. His favorite was *The Coral Island* by R. M. Ballantyne, a Scottish author whose death not long before had prompted an entire generation of British schoolboys to start a fund for the erection of a statue in their favorite author's honor. Eric lost himself again and again in Ballantyne's tale of a trio of boys cast away alone on a remote island and forced to fight for survival with only their courage, skill, and a few tools.

For his eighth birthday Eric received a copy of *Gulliver's Travels* from his mother. He was so excited at the prospect of his birthday that he searched the house the night before until he found the gift-wrapped book, and took it to his bedroom where he stayed up late with it. Jonathan Swift's great story was an adventure tale as well, but even at eight Eric sensed that there was something more to *Gulliver's Travels* than simply the exciting situations and incidents faced by Lemuel Gulliver. It was a book to which he would return over and over again, learning something new from it each time he opened the covers.

In addition to books, Eric enjoyed reading magazines and read them carefully, including the advertisements that crowded their pages. He became increasingly self-conscious about his weight, and when an ad offered a certain cure for chubbiness, Eric entered into a brief correspondence with the advertiser. He dropped the idea when he learned how much it would cost.

Reading, writing, and attending to his pets occupied most of his time. Eric Blair was a child of solitary nature, never bothered by time spent solely in his own company, able to escape when alone into the world of his imagination. He was not terribly good at sports, and felt himself to be something of a misfit. He lived with three women, his mother and his two sisters. Their company did not fully prepare him for the companionship of other boys. For a time he became part of a gang of boys headed by local teenagers, but he was not comfortable in their group, and their enjoyment of rough and tumble, dirty pursuits offended his fastidious nature. He spent more time at home, reading, writing, and watching his animals and his baby sister grow.

In school he proved a good student, bright and quick, capable of concentrating closely on his lessons. He grew distracted only occasionally, fancying himself in love with one or another of the older girls in the school but keeping his infatuations to himself. Mostly, he studied. He understood as well as Ida, it seemed, the importance of education to his future, and knew that it would not be long before he would be sent away to a preparatory school where he would be faced with courses designed to prepare him for public school (as private high schools are known in Britain).

That preparation, in fact, was the goal toward which his early years were directed. Although the Blairs were not wealthy, they held a secure position in the British class system, and a young man of Eric's background could be expected, well before the age of ten, to be sent to a fine preparatory school after which he would attend one of Britain's more prestigious public schools. After that he might go on to Oxford or Cambridge university. Even if a university was not a boy's final destination, he could expect to be in school until he was about nineteen, readying himself for a life in the army or navy, the church, or the colonial service.

By the time Eric was eight, in 1911, the same year Richard Blair retired and returned to Britain, his parents and the nuns at Sunnylands were working together to gain him entry into a good preparatory school. Eric's intelligence was in his favor, for it seemed likely that by virtue of his good grades he would be awarded a scholarship (a reduction in fees) to one of the schools

19

most favored by the wealthy. Before her husband's return, Ida had talked with the nuns at Sunnylands, listened to their recommendations, studied the histories of various schools, and approached her final decision. She was most impressed with St. Cyprian's, a school barely older than the century, which had earned a fine reputation for itself in a short time. It was the sort of place where Eric could meet boys from backgrounds wealthier than his own, connections which might serve him well as he approached adulthood. In addition, St. Cyprian's was respected for the academic excellence it demanded of students. The nuns at Sunnylands felt confident that Eric, with his grades and intelligence, could be awarded a scholarship to St. Cyprian's. Ida traveled to Eastbourne, in Sussex, to inspect the school and to discuss Eric's prospects with its headmaster and his wife, Mr. and Mrs. Vaughan Wilkes.

Such was the nature of social prestige and position in Britain before 1914 and the start of World War I that Mr. and Mrs. Wilkes were as concerned with Eric's meeting their standards as Ida was with the Wilkeses measuring up to hers, if not more so: St. Cyprian's fame had not developed by accident. The school attracted students from the very top classes of British society, and while it was important to take on bright students whose parents were not so well off, the Wilkeses were also aware that there was no shortage of qualified boys from the middle, but not privileged, landed, or titled classes. They wanted the right sort of lad to mix with the children of the nobility and the very wealthy.

Both Ida's and the nuns' recommendation of Eric made a good impression on Mr. and Mrs. Wilkes. The boy was exactly the type they sought, and they offered to accept him beginning with the fall term, 1911, and to reduce the tuition by half. Even so, the Blairs would be facing charges of £90 per school year. Richard Blair's service pension was less than £450, meaning that the boy's schooling would devour more than twenty percent of the family's income; and that was before the additional and unavoidable expenses of clothing, transportation, and incidental money.

Still, Ida was determined to launch her son well, and if the family was careful, the tuition could be worked into their budget. An agreement was reached with the Wilkeses, and it was also decided that Eric would not be told he was a scholarship student. They did not wish Eric to be made still more self-conscious by the knowledge that, relative to some of his new classmates, he was from a poor family.

That summer Richard Blair returned from India, and the family went on a long holiday to the coast. Mingled with the excitement brought by the father's return home was the excitement of the son preparing for departure. Throughout the summer of 1911 Ida remained busy packing and repacking Eric's belongings, checking off items on the list of clothes and other things the boy would need during his first term at school. She made certain she had the requisite number of socks and pajamas for Eric, that the Bible insisted upon by the school was in good condition, that his athletic clothes were in good repair, that his caps fit him snugly. It was quite an undertaking and coupled with the adjustment of having her husband home to stay, it made for a hectic season for Ida Blair.

But as September and the start of term approached, all was in readiness. The contents of Eric's bags matched the lists provided by the Wilkeses. The family had gotten used to having Richard Blair home, although the house was now kept many degrees warmer than was customary, Mr. Blair having become permanently acclimated to the heat of India. Avril was three, toddling everywhere, while Marjorie—herself in a good school, though not one so fine or expensive as St. Cyprian's—was a poised and articulate young woman.

Eric spent the time before departure with his books and his pets, reading, stroking the animals, examining prized issues in his growing stamp collection. He was very quiet; he had nothing much to say. At last September arrived, and the family traveled to London where Eric was to be placed on a train for St. Cyprian's. Other boys bound for the school were at the station, but Eric, shy, said little. He bid his parents farewell and listened solemnly to their final bits of advice. Then he boarded the train to leave home for the first time, careful to keep up his courage, determined to make the most of this adventure. It was, after all, expected of him.

TWO

ST. CYPRIAN'S

WITH AN ENROLLMENT OF fewer than one hundred boys, St. Cyprian's was not a large school. Its facilities consisted of two large, many-roomed houses, under whose roofs all of the school's indoor activities took place. Long hallways lined with doors held dormitory rooms for the students, small rooms and apartments for the faculty, a dining hall, library, chapel, kitchen, and bathrooms. Outside there were spacious lawns and a single playing field that served double duty as the site not only of cricket and soccer matches but also of practice marches, during which the boys learned discipline under the command of the school's drill instructor.

St. Cyprian's had fewer than a dozen teachers, or masters, as they were called, along with Mr. and Mrs. Vaughan Wilkes. The masters were responsible for drilling the boys in a variety of subjects, and the classroom work seemed at times as much forced march and steps by the numbers as did the ranked formations on the field outside. At St. Cyprian's and similar preparatory schools across Britain, the teachers and administrations were less concerned with whether or not the students actually understood the material for which they were responsible than they were with whether or not their charges would be able to give the correct answers on the tests and examinations they would face when seeking entrance to more advanced schools.

The measure of the masters' success was not the spark of intellectual excitement ignited in young minds but the number of students who won high places to the great schools such as Harrow, Winchester, and especially Eton. Good performance on entrance exams was what mattered—performance that would reflect favorably upon St. Cyprian's.

Arriving at the school in September 1911, Eric Arthur Blair, age eight, felt a curious and almost frightening mixture of emotions. The school itself was lovely, with the two huge houses dominating the grounds, which were not far from white chalk cliffs overlooking the English Channel. He was surrounded for the first time in his life by other boys of the same age, though from disparate backgrounds. Some of them were children of nobility, both British and foreign, others were accustomed to great wealth, still others were unknowing scholarship students such as himself. All felt very small as they approached the school, uncertain of what sort of world they were entering.

They learned quickly enough. Under the unwavering guidance of Mr. and Mrs. Vaughan Wilkes, St. Cyprian's had developed a regimen for the boys designed to strengthen their characters, to instill in them the harsh discipline they would need in order to fulfill the obligations their rank in society would impose upon them.

Days began early with a communal plunge into a long, chilly pool, which also served as a bath. The shock of the cold and generally scummy water chased sleep from the boys' minds, and a vigorous toweling stirred their blood, according to the Wilkeses. Breakfast came next, and again following theories held by Mr. and Mrs. Wilkes, the meal was small: too large a breakfast, they felt, might make the boys lazy or sleepy, and there was a day's hard work ahead.

Classes began immediately after breakfast, and Eric learned from the first day that he would find at St. Cyprian's none of the excitement and fun of learning that he had so enjoyed at Sunnylands. He was older now, the masters reminded him, at eight a young man by the standards of British schooling, and his studies served a different purpose. Achievement was the rule of the day, and a person's position in the class rankings was the achievement students should keep foremost in their minds.

As a first-year student, Eric was placed in classes in Latin, French, mathematics, history, and English. He recognized immediately that the men who stood at the head of the class were little interested in him. They had been through it all before, and the world of learning and letters held no further excitement. Rarely would students read an entire book. Rather, a course in literature or history would be composed of those passages and facts most likely to be faced on the examinations that would be the ultimate test of the teachers' achievement. Lessons were taught by rote, with memorization rather than understanding the key to a good grade. It was not what Eric had expected.

Before his first day was finished, Eric was overcome with a wave of homesickness that finally broke through his self-control. He hung his head and began to weep. Mrs. Wilkes spotted the boy and bent at his side, reminding Eric that, like all the other boys, he was to call her "Mum" while he was at St. Cyprian's. She was the wife of the headmaster, and she was one of the teachers, she said, but she also wanted to be the source of maternal comfort when it was called for. She took Eric into her arms and held him tightly, but the comfort she offered was not the sort the boy desired.

Mrs. Wilkes dominated school life far more than did her husband. She was constantly on patrol, walking up and down the halls in search not only of boys in need of consolation, but also alert for transgressions of the school's strict rules. St. Cyprian's instilled maturity in its students, and the students were *expected* to display maturity from the day they arrived. Anything less was a denial of their class and of their responsibilities. St. Cyprian's was typical of such schools for the middle classes.

Eric Blair had no wish to deny his responsibilities. He endeavored to be an example of the mature young man that Mum

Wilkes and the masters so frequently described as the ideal toward which he should aspire. But everything was so different. Where Ida Blair had transformed even common vegetables into tasty and appetizing casseroles and dishes, the food at St. Cyprian's was poorly cooked and often tasted spoiled. The home in which Eric had passed his childhood was kept clean and neat, but conditions at St. Cyprian's were generally filthy, from the scum on the surface of the bathwater to the crusts of dried food that had to be chipped from plates and utensils before they could be used. Where his home life and the adventure stories he read had led him to believe that the future—including St. Cyprian's—held challenges to which a well-prepared boy could rise and over which he could triumph, the thrust of the teaching at St. Cyprian's seemed to be that one's life was always poised on the edge of danger, that failure lurked everywhere, and that one must constantly be on guard against it.

Before he had been at St. Cyprian's a month, Eric wet his bed. To Mrs. Wilkes, to her husband, and to the staff of masters, bed-wetting stood among the most grievous of offenses against not only nature but against society itself. Incontinence bespoke a lack of self-control, it revealed the hidden flaws in Eric's character, it was an inexcusable demonstration of the boy's lack of maturity. He was called to Headmaster Wilkes's office and told of these truths, and reminded in no uncertain terms of the punishment that lay ahead if he failed to control himself and his bladder.

It did not help. The next night, Eric wet his bed again, and awoke the next morning to find himself summoned once more to face the headmaster and receive from that voice of authority the lecture on how Eric had failed, once more, to measure up. He would be given another chance but not, it was made clear, as an indulgence, but because he, a bright boy, should be able to bring himself under control. That, after all, was what St. Cyprian's and the education it offered were all about: control of mind, control of manners, control of emotions, control of body.

Eric tried, but his body refused to cooperate, and, waking yet again to sodden sheets, he knew without being told that the time of warnings had passed. For this offense, for the repetition of that offense, he must be punished, not simply scolded. It was obvious to Headmaster and Mrs. Wilkes that words alone would not reach the boy. An example must be set for him.

Following afternoon tea, at which guests from the community were occasionally present, Mrs. Wilkes beckoned Eric to remain behind. The other boys left the dining hall, and Eric approached Mrs. Wilkes and an unfamiliar woman who sat at her table. He stared at Mrs. Wilkes and recalled that she had, not long after his first bout of homesickness, taken him and some other students on a picnic. It had not been the gay sort of picnic that Eric had enjoyed with his mother, though it had evidently been intended as such. Eric thought also of the nickname the older boys had given Mum Wilkes—they called her "Flip," in crude reference to the motion of her ample bosom as she strode down the halls. The older boys were continually making vulgar jokes such as that, as well as picking on the younger, smaller, weaker boys such as Eric.

Now, in the dining hall after tea, Mrs. Wilkes introduced Eric to her companion, although he did not catch the woman's name. He nodded at her, seeking to be polite but not quite daring to speak. Mrs. Wilkes rattled on a bit, referring to Eric occasionally, building up to the moment when, in a conversational tone of voice as though discussing something so matter of fact as gardening, she told her companion that Eric Blair was the eight-year-old who could not keep from wetting his bed.

Eric was stunned, but he managed to retain his composure. He would not give in and let Mrs. Wilkes enjoy the humiliation she had forced upon him. Nor did Mrs. Wilkes stop speaking. She chatted, while the other woman nodded in agreement, about how deplorable a thing it was for a boy of Eric's years to soil his sheets at night. It was a failure, certainly, and one which *would no longer be tolerated.* Should the offense occur again, she said, as much to her companion as to Eric, the boy would be turned over to the bigger students for a sound beating. Should it happen again, she said, that was all the boy would deserve. With that, she dismissed Eric, and he walked from the dining hall, conscious with every step of Mrs. Wilkes and the other woman staring at him as he left, talking about him as he departed.

And that night he wet his bed once more.

Next morning, rather than being turned over to the older boys for his beating, Eric was summoned to Headmaster Wilkes's office. Mr. Wilkes was a man of medium size, whose rounded shoulders and broad face made him seem larger than he really was. Even a small man, though, would tower over a boy of eight, and on the morning of Eric's punishment, Mr. Wilkes did tower over the boy, bending to stare at him from his vantage point and intoning once more the now familiar lecture. It was bad enough—unforgivable!—to wet one's bed, but to continue to do so was evidence of much more than mere incontinence. Such repetition was evidence of a rebellious and defiant nature and must be dealt with corporally: nothing less than physical punishment would do. Eric was told to prepare himself for a caning.

The cane used by the Headmaster was likely of bamboo, although Eric would remember it as having been a heavy, ivory-handled riding crop. Whatever the implement, its use was quickly made clear as Eric bent and braced himself, and Wilkes stood straight and raised the cane above his head and brought it down hard on Eric's back. The boy did not cry out; it was as though he had decided to prove by his lack of emotion that he *did* have control over himself and his body. He endured the caning stoically, drawing his breath as the cane rose, holding his breath as the cane sliced air on its downward arc to bite into his back. The punishment seemed to last forever, and Eric would later claim that in the midst of the beating the riding crop, as he remembered it, broke, its ivory handle flying across the room, angering Mr. Wilkes even further. Eric never cried and did not even come close to requesting mercy. He could take whatever the headmaster offered and would prove by his silence the character he knew he possessed.

When the punishment was at last ended, Eric assured Mr. Wilkes that he had truly learned his lesson and would no longer wet his bed. He was dismissed. Outside Headmaster Wilkes's office a group of boys waited, eager to hear the details of Eric's beating. Eric stood tall as he emerged from the office, and with a smirk of pride he told his classmates that the caning had not been all that bad—it hadn't hurt at all, really. His back was tougher than Wilkes's blows. Eric's brave proclamation was greeted with wonder by the boys but with anger by Mum Wilkes, who, unfortunately, happened to be passing by and overheard Eric's boast.

Such defiance was as evil as bed-wetting and could no more be tolerated than that other offense. She took Eric and marched him immediately back into the headmaster's office, where he was ordered to bend once more and receive instruction from the edge of a cane. This beating was even more ferocious, and during it Eric learned a lesson. What mattered, he realized, was for Wilkes to think that his message had gotten through. Eric collapsed weeping, crying out that he had learned his lesson, had seen the error of his ways. He knew now, he said, how bad a little boy he had been, and knew how hard he must work to become a good young man. His tears made their point, for the caning soon ceased, and he was dismissed.

That night Eric again wet his bed, and the next morning he was summoned after breakfast to Headmaster Wilkes's office for another sound beating. Eric told no one, but this session under the cane hurt no more than had the first. It was as though he had willed himself to feel nothing once the punishment began. He had not forgotten the most important lesson, which was to let the headmaster know clearly that a lesson had been learned and learned painfully. Eric wept dutifully, apologized, was dismissed, and never again wet his bed.

There were other lessons as he adjusted to the rhythms of the school, and other pieces of understanding to be put into practice. When he wrote to his parents, for example, he never mentioned his punishment or let on to any unhappiness at all. In part this was boyish pride: he wanted them to see how well he could fend for himself. There was also a feeling at St. Cyprian's that the boys' mail was closely scrutinized by Mum Wilkes, and that comments which reflected poorly upon the school would not only be censored, but would also bring down punishment on the correspondent. Eric's letters home were brief and chatty, telling of his studies, mentioning proudly the standing he earned in each of his classes, occasionally requesting items left at home such as his stamp collection.

The cheerful schoolboy of the letters was a pose, however, as was the weeping boy prostrate at the feet of the headmaster. Eric Blair, in the company of young boys for the first time in his life, learned of his own nature by watching them. He loved books and reading, but most of the other boys loathed such scholarly activities. They loved rough-and-tumble sports, but Eric was awkward. He tumbled more often than he displayed grace or agility, and often cost points to the teams to which he was assigned. He was not the sort of boy immediately chosen for a team, his performance hindering that of his teammates. The others seemed lithe and limber, making Eric ever more self-conscious of his own chubbiness. He felt that he smelled bad. His lungs rebelled as winter approached, and he found himself going often to the infirmary where he lay alone in bed; he made no real friends and thus had few visitors when he was confined to the sickroom. And when he was up and about he found himself the target of bullying assaults by older boys. More than once his nose or lips were bloodied by an unexpected, unwarranted blow—but it did no good to complain to the staff. Such complaints were, like bed-wetting or homesickness, signs of weakness, expressions of flawed character.

The one area in which he might hope to find some escape from his loneliness was the classroom. His standings confirmed his brightness. He had not been at St. Cyprian's long before establishing himself at or near the top of every class he took. Learning came easily to him, and not only the memorization and rote learning that was the school's sole educational theory. Eric also revealed a natural gift for comprehension and understanding. He could make connections between the ideas presented by the masters and begin to trace the flow of ideas through history, to observe and recapitulate their rise and fall over the centuries. He proved himself equally adept with words, his early appreciation of poetry growing deeper as he was exposed to Shakespeare, to the classical Greek and Roman poets, and to other great works of literature. At age eight he knew already, and told those around him, that he would be a writer when he was grown.

Such pronouncements fell on deaf ears. To his hardy classmates, Eric's love of books and reading was one more indication of his weakness. The masters were not even that interested. Generally underpaid, genuinely devoid of scholarly habits, they cared little for this boy's brightness and rarely took the trouble to compliment or even respond to his insights. Eric grew more withdrawn.

Mr. and Mrs. Wilkes did notice that Eric, for all the trouble he had given them early on, was an exceptionally intelligent boy. Such boys were prized at schools such as St. Cyprian's, for they were most likely to earn scholarships to good schools, and the number of St. Cyprian's graduates accepted by Eton, for example, would help the Wilkeses attract students in the future. They took to meeting with Eric occasionally, reminding him of the greatness he could achieve by excelling at his schoolwork, and encouraged him to study even harder, making certain that he kept at his books. For all that, though, even they had little interest in any originality of thought the boy displayed. Originality, after all, was virtually another form of rebellion.

The first term dragged by and Eric was delighted to return to Henley for the Christmas holidays. It took a bit of adjusting to grow accustomed to warm, large breakfasts in which he did not first have to search for hairs. It was special once more to have a room to himself, and a bed with enough blankets. And above all it felt wonderful to be surrounded once more by family rather than strangers. Richard Blair, in his midfifties now, might be aloof and more than a bit stuffy, guided by habits developed over a regimented career in the colonies. Nonetheless, he was *father*, and could be counted on for companionship during riverside walks, occasional fishing outings, and lovely surprises such as pocketknives. Ida Blair percolated with enthusiasm and good humor, her colorful clothes and bright earrings adding life as she darted here and there, rarely still, a good cook and a caring nurse, *mother*. Marjorie was special, too, not only as a sister but also as someone with whom Eric could share his love of books. And Avril, the baby of the family, was growing rapidly; a special bond developed between Eric and his younger sister. They cared for the family's pets together, Eric protective and instructive with the little girl. Holidays were fine times, but they always ended too quickly.

Back at St. Cyprian's early in 1912, Eric found himself once more alone, and, he increasingly felt, ostracized. Eric Blair did not fit in, and no one was more aware of that than Eric Blair himself. He came to dread rousing each morning to face the rows of filthy sinks, the toilet stalls whose doors could not be locked, the plunge and swim through the murky pool that was the only bath the boys had, dressing beside other boys who were muscular while he was chubby. Mealtimes were disgusting, the already low quality of the food declining even farther as winter deepened.

Classes themselves were a horror: Eric was smarter than the other boys and that did nothing to help him make friends. To encourage competition among the students—competition which built character, according to Mr. and Mrs. Wilkes—the boys' class standings were posted each week, and each week Eric Blair's name stood near the top of the roster for his courses. Those high marks made him an easy target for less bright, more bullying boys.

He was a target of laughter as well: in athletic competitions he was as untalented as it was possible to be. When his teams lost, the losses were blamed on Eric. When, on occasion, a team on which he was a member won, he shared little of the credit. The only athletic events he enjoyed were the infrequent visits to large public pools in nearby Eastbourne, but even in the water he did not excel as a competitor. He mustered what energy he could for the sports and even managed some enthusiasm, but he was not an athlete. His body conspired against him. As a result of a midwinter iceskating expedition, Eric's lungs acted up once more, and he watched much of the winter pass from the vantage point of an infirmary bed.

The winter did pass, though, and the spring, and Eric Blair's first year at St. Cyprian's was nearly behind him. For his ninth birthday in June, his parents sent him a watch, and he wore it everywhere. He watched the calendar as well, counting the days until he could return to Henley for the summer, seizing upon every distraction to take his mind from St. Cyprian's. One day there was a shipwreck within sight of the coast, and the boys spent hours watching the ship go down. As the weather improved, walks across the area's fields occupied afternoons. And, late in the school year, Eric briefly enjoyed a moment's triumph on the playing field, scoring an important goal almost by accident.

The summer of 1912 was spent with his family and his pets. Eric passed a great deal of his vacation reading and told Marjorie more than once that he would be a writer. That fall, after he had returned to St. Cyprian's, the Blair family moved from Henley to a larger house with more spacious grounds in Shiplake, barely two miles away. The new house was quickly named "Roselawn" by Ida Blair, and the more suburban setting agreed with the family. Eric wrote often to ask if his pets had survived the move in good health.

At St. Cyprian's the best thing he could say for his second year was that the school no longer held any surprises for him. The food was still terrible, the washrooms still smelly and dirty, the classes still stultifyingly dull. One high point of the year was a costume party which Eric attended dressed—in a school costume—as a regal footman. He enjoyed wearing the red velvet coat and red silk trousers; a white waistcoat and white wig completed the costume. The party was a colorful incident in a year otherwise as dull and drab as had been the first. Eric's athletic performance improved somewhat, and his class standings remained high.

The summer of 1913 was spent in Shiplake. Roselawn sat in the center of nearly an acre of land, and Eric, Marjorie, and Avril walked the grounds often, taking great interest in the variety of flowers and animal life to be found there. The family menagerie now included birds as well as terriers and kittens, rabbits and guinea pigs, and Eric divided his holiday time between the animals and books.

In the fall, Eric's third year at St. Cyprian's began, and upon arrival at school the boy's studiousness and natural academic talent were rewarded. He was placed in the school's scholarship class, an advanced and challenging section whose students seemed most likely to win scholarships to Eton, Harrow, or one of the other great British schools. Great pressure was placed upon the students: the temper and tone of the instruction was the same as in regular classes—memorization, recitation, drill—but the volume of work assigned was far greater. Scholarship class students were expected to yield their holidays to the school, studying while the other boys played. Vacations were likewise crammed with assignments. Eric might return home for a few days and carry with him an assignment consisting of hundreds of lines of poetry to be memorized, long charts of historical dates to learn by rote, dozens upon dozens of French and Latin verbs to conjugate.

He rose to the challenges, aware that excellence was now expected of him. His class standings remained high, and he also managed to continue his outside reading. From the masters he received instruction in important or noteworthy passages from English and classical Greek and Latin literature; on his own he encountered novels and plays as entities, studying the ways in which authors developed their characters and themes.

That year at St. Cyprian's, Eric made a true friend, a new boy who shared his precocious love and understanding of literature. Cyril Connolly, like Eric Blair, knew from an early age that he wanted to become a writer, and also like Eric, he spent every free moment immersed in a book. Eric and Cyril Connolly took to each other instantly, comparing favorite books, introducing each other to books that might otherwise have been overlooked. And they began sharing stories that they created themselves, taking the trouble to criticize each other's work as well as enjoy it.

Eric returned to the Blair home in Shiplake for the summer of 1914. He took with him long lists of academic tasks that must be accomplished before the resumption of classes, but he also found time for fun. One afternoon, early in the summer, while walking through fields near his home, he noticed children from a nearby house playing beside the fence that surrounded their lawn. Eric immediately bent and placed his hands and head on the ground and heaved his feet into the air. He balanced precariously until one of the children asked *why* he was standing on his head. His purpose accomplished, Eric righted himself and pointed out that people standing on their heads were more quickly noticed by those around them—just as he had been.

The children were named Buddicom, and they were close in age to the Blair children. Jacintha, the eldest, was thirteen, two years older than Eric, and her brother, Prosper, was, at ten, a year younger. A third child, Guinever, called Guiny, was seven years old, a year older than Avril Blair. All in all it seemed from the first as though a family of friends had been fashioned for the Blair children, and the friendships that were struck that first afternoon deepened as the summer passed.

Eric became especially close to Jacintha Buddicom. She shared his love of books, and like Cyril Connolly at St. Cyprian's, enjoyed talking of the sort of life a writer could fashion. She and Eric even discussed the bindings which would be most

35

handsome when publishers began assembling "collected editions" of their works. When not talking of the stories and poems they would one day write, Eric and Jacintha put their fascination with language to work creating games. They invented a poetry game in which words selected at random were fashioned into nonsense verses; they became masters of more traditional word games such as Hangman; they even spent long hours inventing words of their own—odd-sounding words that did not exist but were clever enough that the children felt they should.

Words were not their sole preoccupation. On clear days Eric, Jacintha, and the other children would set out on long expeditions through open fields, spotting animals, selecting flowers to be pressed in books, collecting birds' eggs—no more than one egg from each nest—for their collections. Jacintha's father had been a museum curator, and his concern for orderliness and proper cataloging carried over to his children. It was a concern which they shared with the young Blairs, and their coins, stamps, flowers, and colorful birds' eggs were displayed neatly, each item clearly labeled and identified.

Despite such pleasant distractions, Eric kept up with his school assignments, but when he returned to St. Cyprian's for the fall term, 1914, he found the already intense pressure of the special scholarship class had increased. He was eleven now, approaching the age when his mastery of the required curriculum would be tested not by disinterested masters at St. Cyprian's, but by the more exacting members of the entrance boards at Eton, Harrow, and Wellington. The dozens of historical facts and dates, hundreds of lines of classical poetry, and thousands of Latin, Greek, and French words Eric had already memorized were mere preparation for the academic agenda he and the other scholarship class students now faced. While other students played, they studied; when other students traveled home for holidays, the scholarship class remained in Eastbourne for drill and repetition. Eric nonetheless found time to read books of his own selection, often staying up after curfew to steal a few hours with a book by H. G. Wells or William Thackeray. He was taken with the ways in which Thackeray made his characters and the Victorian world in which they lived come alive. And for years there were few writers whose works he relished more than those of Wells. Eric, reading clandestinely in the small hours of night, could hardly stop turning the pages of Wells's romances of science, utopias, and the future.

The real world of the present intruded upon the lives of the students at St. Cyprian's that fall. On August 4, 1914, Great Britain had declared war on Germany, and over the course of the next few weeks Europe became engulfed in the First World War. The practice marches on St. Cyprian's fields took on more meaning as Eric and the other students thought of their fellows, most of them but a few years older than the students themselves, marching off to fight and die in the muddy battlefields of the war. For Eric, the eruption of war served as a muse to his poetic streak, and before the conflict was two months old he had written a poem which his mother thought sufficiently skilled to submit for publication to a local newspaper.

Awake Young Men of England

Oh! give me the strength of the Lion
The wisdom of Reynard the Fox
And then I'll hurl troops at the Germans
And give them the hardest of knocks.

Oh! think of the War lord's mailed fist,
That is striking at England today:
And think of the lives that our soldiers
Are fearlessly throwing away.

Awake! Oh you young men of England,
For if when your country's in need,
You do not enlist by the thousand,
You truly are cowards indeed.

Ida Blair mailed Eric's poem to the *Henley and South Oxfordshire Standard* where its quality—especially for an author not yet twelve years old—was recognized. The newspaper printed the poem early in October 1914.

Its appearance in print delighted Eric, and he was even more delighted with the response that publication won him from Mr. and Mrs. Wilkes. The entire student body was assembled and Mrs. Wilkes read the poem aloud, taking care for once to single Eric Blair out for praise rather than criticism. The pleasant mood did not last, though. Eric was discovered reading a forbidden book. It was a realistic novel, *Sinister Street,* by Scottish novelist Compton Mackenzie, which was considered scandalously racy. He was placed once more under the headmaster's cane.

Far worse punishment awaited him as he moved through the last two years at St. Cyprian's. Although Eric felt that he never truly became "one of the boys" and recognized both his lack of athletic talent and his deeper commitment to the world of ideas, he did not think of himself as less than his fellows as a person. That would change when, during a period of hard studying and growing academic burdens, Eric's performance in the scholarship class slipped a bit. He was summoned to Headmaster Wilkes's office, as he had been summoned so many times before, but this visit was not to include the bite of the headmaster's cane.

Wilkes invited Eric to sit, pointed out to him that his recent declining performance was unsatisfactory and could not be tolerated, and then, without warning, revealed that Eric was attending St. Cyprian's on scholarship, telling the boy of the reduced fee arrangement he had struck with Ida Blair. Did Eric wish to betray the confidence of his parents by failing to excel in school? Wilkes described them as living in far more reduced financial circumstances than was actually the case. Had Wilkes been mistaken in awarding Eric a scholarship? Did the boy have no gratitude? Could he not appreciate the *charity* which St. Cyprian's had shown such a poor lad?

Charity? Poor lad? Eric left Wilkes's office shattered by the lecture. He had never thought of himself as poor—and the Blair family was not poor—nor had he really thought of boys from wealthier families as rich. At St. Cyprian's they had come to seem essentially similar, some more talented as athletes, others more skilled at study, but still boys with common interests and concerns. Now, walking the halls of the school, Eric realized that there had been differences all along. Some students had more pocket money than others; some had finer clothes; some carried themselves more nobly, or obviously had received instruction from more mannered families or understood social lines more clearly. And Eric Blair? It was, he thought to himself, much as Headmaster Wilkes had said: he was a poor boy who must make his way in the world on the sufferance and indulgence of others. If he did not succeed in winning a scholarship he would be cast out into the world to survive—or more likely, Wilkes had said, to fail miserably—on his own.

Eric took stock of himself and realized that Wilkes, at least within the confines of St. Cyprian's, was correct. The only device Eric had in his favor was a fine memory and an alert mind. His grades climbed once more and he settled into a routine he loathed. He spent his final two years cramming his mind with facts, figures, and quotations that he would regurgitate for the examination boards.

In Europe the war entered its years of stalemate, British and French troops facing Germans from trenches separated by muddy, body-strewn fields. Hundreds of thousands of young men died to gain a few feet of territory. Eric and his classmates often visited local hospitals, carrying cigarettes and candy to wounded soldiers. Football had been replaced by longer drills and rifle practice. Eric became a good shot, able to hit both stationary and moving targets. As a result of wartime shortages, the food at St. Cyprian's became even more disgusting than it had been before, and the meager servings became even smaller. Wartime deprivations exerted their influence on every aspect of British life, and the war years seemed one dreary, endless winter. Awake young men of England, indeed.

Shortages imposed by the war affected the home life of the Blairs as well. They moved from Roselawn, with its acre of land, to a smaller house whose yard seemed barely large enough to stand in. When he was home for vacation Eric could not wait to leave the cramped house and set out with Jacintha and Prosper Buddicom for a day in the fields. An uncle had given Eric a rifle for Christmas, and Eric put it to use shooting birds and small animals. Jacintha was horrified that Eric and Prosper took such joy in killing, but she could do little to dissuade them. Prosper kept a record of every successful hunt, and he and Eric planned more and more ambitious jaunts after game. Once they killed a hedgehog, packed it in clay, and attempted to bake it in the Buddicoms' kitchen, greatly angering not only Jacintha but the Buddicoms' cook, who had to clean up the mess. Not long afterward, Eric and Prosper began experimenting with chemistry, particularly the chemistry of fermentation, and the still they constructed in the Buddicom's kitchen exploded, scattering glass and splashing liquid everywhere. The cook would not clean this mess; she had quit.

Eric said nothing to his family or to Jacintha about Wilkes's cruel lecture. The perception of himself as poor settled in for a while, and left its mark upon Eric's thoughts, but it was not the sort of thing he would talk about. For one thing, early in 1915, Jacintha's father abandoned his family and emigrated to Australia, and Eric was well aware of the pain the desertion caused his friends. How could he complain of poverty when they had no father? For another, he began to develop a method of coping with the sense of inadequacy Wilkes had attempted to foster. Eric became increasingly assertive, made more and more statements about the fame he would win as a writer, even managing to sneer at those who felt themselves better than he. He did not need, he made clear to Connolly at St. Cyprian's and to his Buddicom friends in Shiplake, to be popular or well liked. He would be *great*, author of "collected editions," and that would be enough.

Fall 1915 passed quickly, and then Eric was into his final season at St. Cyprian's. Entrance examinations for the coveted public school scholarships would begin early in 1916, and Eric was clearly well prepared for them. He dutifully sat in classes, answering correctly when queried by a master, expressing disinterest otherwise. Politic performance no longer mattered: Wilkes could not hurt him now. The examinations were beginning and by their results—one way or another—Eric would be gone from St. Cyprian's before the end of the school year.

In February, Eric took the examinations for Wellington, which had a high reputation—though no school's reputation was so high as Eton's—but which prepared its graduates for army careers. Eric passed the Wellington examination easily, and returned to St. Cyprian's for a final round of cramming before the Eton exams.

In June Eric and Mr. Wilkes traveled to Eton for the examinations, which lasted nearly three days. Competition was, as expected, fierce. The scholarship Eric sought was that of King's Scholar, and it was from the King's Scholarships, established by Henry VI in the fifteenth century, that the great college had developed. Henry VI had created the position of King's Scholar and the school that the scholars would attend to give deserving young men, regardless of class, the opportunity of a fine education. King's Scholars were charged only nominal tuition, far less in fact than even the half-rate fees Eric's parents had paid for St. Cyprian's. Academic excellence was the sole criterion for a King's Scholar: a class—or election, as it was called—of King's Scholars might theoretically be composed of students of the humblest families in Britain as well as the noblest. Each year there was room at Eton for an election of only a dozen or so boys, so position on the examinations was crucial to entry.

For two-and-a-half days Eric sat through tests of his memory for obscure facts, his knowledge of literature, his abilities with foreign languages. One of his examinations was interrupted with the news that Lord Kitchener, the great British hero of Egypt and Britain's War Minister, had been killed when the ship on which he was traveling on a secret mission to Russia had struck a mine and sunk. The news was a shock. Kitchener was one of the great military leaders of Britain, and was even more important as a wartime symbol, but the exams were not canceled. Eric pressed on, doing his best and confident that his performance was good indeed. At last he and Wilkes returned to St. Cyprian's.

As he waited to discover whether or not Eton lay in his future, Eric returned to public poetry, this time with a composition, assigned by Mum Wilkes, to commemorate Kitchener's death.

Kitchener

No stone is set to mark his nation's loss
No stately tomb enshrines his noble breast;
Not e'en the tribute of a wooden cross
Can mark his hero's rest.

He needs them not, his name untarnished stands,
Remindful of the mighty deeds he worked,
Footprints of one, upon time's changeful sands,
Who ne'er his duty shirked.

Who follows in his steps no danger shuns,
Nor stoops to conquer by shameful deed,
An honest and unselfish race he runs,
From fear and malice freed.

Once more Eric's gift for poetic expression won favor from Mrs. Wilkes. His new poem was read to the assembled school, his patriotism applauded by the administration. Again he saw his name in print in the Henley newspaper, where the poem appeared late in July.

A less fortunate publication came earlier. When the results of the King's Scholars examinations were tabulated, Eric Blair had earned fourteenth place among all the applicants. Each year's election, though, was determined by the number of spaces available in King's College at Eton, and in 1916 it had room for barely a dozen scholars. He'd done well, but not well enough to enter Eton in 1916. There was some hope, though, that as young men left Eton to serve in the war, room might be made for the addition of a few boys to the 1916 election.

Meanwhile, Eric faced a decision about his future. He had been accepted on scholarship to Wellington. It was agreed that he would enter that school early in 1917. A final season, then, awaited him at St. Cyprian's.

Eric felt liberated. While he did not actually cross the line between diffidence and defiance, his behavior at school in the fall of 1916 made clear to Mr. and Mrs. Wilkes that their fears about the boy had not been groundless. With his examinations past and passed, Eric became lazy in the classroom, occasionally producing the right answer, but more often than not, never volunteering. He made mock of his patriotic poetry, and on more than one occasion of patriotism itself. He, who had placed high on one of Britain's most rigorous scholarship examinations, now expressed his disdain for study or hard work of any academic sort. He was going to be a poet, a *writer,* and the doctrinaire, mundane approaches to literature as practiced by the Wilkeses and their staff simply struck him as foolish.

When the Christmas holidays arrived, Eric left St. Cyprian's for the last time. His farewells to Mr. Wilkes and to Mum Wilkes were cool and restrained. He had been in their care for more than five years, and he had nothing to offer them other than a polite handshake. Eric Blair had, however, taken from them what he could: a hatred for unquestioning obedience to authority, a loathing of rote learning and memorization for its own sake, and a sense of awareness that class and social position counted for a great deal in the world but that, for those not born to high class or position, there was not a great deal that could be done. Eric might hate authority, but authority existed; it was a fact of life that must be faced. As he grew older Eric would have to come to terms with the nature of authority, and of his response to it. Mr. Wilkes felt confident that Eric would fail at whatever he attempted. As he left St. Cyprian's, Eric Blair was full of hope, but not at all certain that he would be able to disprove Mr. Wilkes's charge.

THREE

ERIC AT ETON

ERIC BLAIR ARRIVED AT Wellington College early in 1917. He was still disappointed that he had failed to win a position in the 1916 election at Eton, but this feeling was tempered somewhat by the excitement of attending Wellington. It was, after all, a school at which he expected to be treated as an adult and to be given more responsibility for his actions than he'd enjoyed at St. Cyprian's. It was an educational institution where, at last, he would receive an *education*. He expected his teachers and classmates to share his own sense of intellectual adventure. Wellington, Eric was certain, would be a place at which the community of ideas, rather than St. Cyprian's community of obedience, would dominate daily life.

He was to be disappointed once more. Eric began to see the reality of the students' situation at Wellington the moment he arrived and started unpacking his belongings. Where he had anticipated a comfortable and cozy private room, he found a small, bare, cold cubicle hardly separated from other similar cubicles. There was no more privacy at Wellington than at the Wilkes's school. His eager expectation of scholarly discussions faded as well. At Wellington the emphasis was upon the preparation of young men for the military, and the curriculum was bent toward that end. Ideas tended to be discussed in ways that would be useful to commanders of soldiers, not masters of words. Before his first week was out, Eric surrendered his preconceptions, accepted the nature of Wellington, and set his course of action. That course was one of relaxation, independent reading, which did little to help his academic performance, and that diffidence toward the school's expectations of him that he had practiced so well during his last term at St. Cyprian's. As class standings were posted, Eric Blair's name was invariably in the midrange. He had no interest in excelling at Wellington.

Still, he was accomplishing enough to get by, if little more than that. He saw the years of school stretching ahead of him and envisioned his Wellington career: nothing exceptional, nothing outstanding, just average or below average performance. He would go through the motions of being a Wellington student, nothing more.

Barely two months of this dull, militaristic existence had passed, however, when Eric learned that he would be able to attend Eton after all. While elections continued to be limited to only a few Scholars, the demand of the war for young men was drawing many of the older students from Eton. As they departed to be commissioned in the services, their places at Eton were filled by students who'd done well on the qualifying examinations. Eric, with his fourteenth placing on the King's Scholar exams, was notified in the spring of 1917 that Eton was ready to have him join its classes.

Eric himself was more than ready. He may have gotten into Eton on the coattails of another's uniform, but he had gotten in, and could not wait to get started. He arrived at Eton in May 1917, a King's Scholar, once more filled with intellectual expectations, a young man at last certain that he was entering an institution that valued the idea of education.

His first few days at Eton fulfilled his hopes. King's Scholars lived in the oldest of Eton's stately buildings, in recognition of the part each generation of Scholars had played in an educational tradition nearly five centuries old. Again, Eric had expected a comfortable private room befitting a Scholar, but his expectations were denied: King's Scholars were each given a cubicle scarcely larger than those at Wellington, whose walls rose barely six feet, with a gap between the top of the wall and the high ceiling. Voices carried from one cubicle to the next; privacy was virtually nonexistent. Nor were the cubicles warm: each wing of the Scholars' quarters held a long common room with a central fireplace; other than that, the students shivered.

It was possible, though, to be warmed by inner fires, and Eric's excitement served him well as he began his career at Eton. He knew that Eton was more than simply a great school—Etonians formed a social community of their own within the British social class system. Etonians could be counted upon to help each other out, forming a not quite unofficial network of contacts and privileges. Position within the Etonian order had to be earned, however, and for each new election there was a barrage of hazings and initiation rites imposed by the upperclassmen. One of his first evenings at Eton, Eric, at an upperclassman's behest, had to stand on a table in the midst of the evening meal and sing at the top of his lungs a rather bawdy American song. He managed to overcome his customary shyness and gave the song a sufficiently energetic rendition—his performance was applauded. Those who sang less well became targets for food, books, and other projectiles hurled by the upper classmen as demonstration of their criticism.

Eric was less fortunate when it came to the, again traditional, beatings administered by older students. The members of each new election faced bruises from the fists of their elders—the beatings were as much a part of Etonian tradition as the small rooms and ancient buildings. There was nothing to be done about the incidents, other than to hope that they occurred infrequently and that the upperclassmen would choose to be at least somewhat merciful. Eric, though fourteen years old, remained short, and his slight stature seemed to provoke the older students. Like his fellow members of the election of 1916, Eric bore the beatings in silence, understanding that his bruises were

47

symbols of a social ritual and the beatings symbols of an Etonian's coming of age. But he and his fellows began talking more and more among themselves of how they would change the cruel practices as they became upperclassmen themselves.

Academically, Eton was closer to the ideal school Eric envisioned than Wellington had been, and his classes were infinitely superior to those he had endured at St. Cyprian's. He was enrolled as a classics major, immersing himself in the great works and languages of the ancient world. The students' days began at 7:30, not with breakfast but with an hour of classes, boys leaping from their beds, bathing hurriedly, donning their uniforms, and seating themselves for concentration before many of them were well awake. After a brief breakfast—scarcely less meager than the morning meal at St. Cyprian's—the students returned to class for three hours of group study, which was followed by a session of one hour with a tutor.

Eric's tutor was A. S. F. Gow, a classics scholar who sought not only to have his students memorize important works, but also to awaken the boys to the artistic and intellectual greatness of the Greek and Roman writers they studied. Gow was a brilliant man and a great teacher who made a favorable impression upon Eric. As he grew to know Gow better, Eric revealed his interest in writing, and although Gow maintained that Blair had no future as a creative writer, he did acknowledge the boy's ability to write stories with morals. Eric worked hard during his first months at Eton on a variety of short pieces, each of which built toward a succinct moral lesson, as did many of the classical pieces he studied.

Classics were not the only elements of Eric's curriculum. As a specialist—as those studying classics were called—he spent seven classroom hours each week studying Latin, and another six studying Greek, but he was also responsible for three hours each in French and mathematics, two hours of classes in English, and an hour of divinity. Classroom and tutorial sessions were only preparation, however, for the long hours of individual study and memorization expected of the boys in the evenings and on holidays.

Three afternoons were set aside from each week for athletic endeavors. Sports, and the sportsmanship and lessons of proper conduct learned on the playing fields, held even more importance at Eton than they had at St. Cyprian's. Etonians were expected to be fierce competitors, both on the playing fields and in their classrooms. Excellence at athletics mattered greatly and exercised an important and unavoidable effect upon one's standing at Eton, in the eyes of the administration and of one's classmates. Detailed diaries were kept recording team performance in each game.

Eric's athletic performance at Eton was as poor as it had been at St. Cyprian's. He lacked the natural grace of the other boys, and could not master the coordination necessary to boot a soccer ball accurately toward a goal, or swing a cricket bat for a solid hit. He did not even run well. The sports diaries soon grew full of neatly recorded comments on Eric Blair's poor showings, many of the records blaming Eric for lost games and the loss of honor that accompanied defeats. He'd sung with enough proficiency to escape mockery during the hazings, but he could not escape humiliation during sporting events. Gradually he gave up even trying to play, accepting for himself the dubious distinction of being the worst athlete among his election, and, according to some of his classmates, working hard to enhance that reputation.

As the school year deepened, Eric's performance in the classroom began to sink toward a level nearly as dismal as his performance on the field. It was as though, having studied and crammed to win his appointment as a King's Scholar, Eric felt he had done enough. He began to be known as a complainer, telling the others in no uncertain terms that the offerings of their teachers were of little use to a man with an independent turn of mind. He would not be content to be one of the old Etonians who went through their years there by the book, blindly following the dictates of tradition and expectation. He took to going out of his way to say shocking, unconventional things, often using crude and undignified language. Among the objects of his disdain were, suddenly, his parents. In discussions with the other boys he listened as they spoke of their parents' achievements, then studied their faces as he spoke rudely of Richard and Ida Blair. They knew nothing, they were provincial in their outlook, their minds were dull and uninformed. Eric became more and more provocative, attacking not only his parents' provincialism, as he saw it, but also the doctrinaire thoughts and minds of his classmates. Even the great classical writers they studied came under disparaging attack as Eric worked to develop his reputation as a rebel and an iconoclast. He was, he showed the others, *different.*

For one thing, he was more intelligent, in many ways, than other boys of his age. Certainly he was well read, and his fine, accurate memory gave him the advantage in debate of invoking writers and quotations to prove his points. Little response was possible, for the other fourteen-year-olds had not read so widely as had Eric, and were less interested in putting ideas together in new ways than they were in acquiring information that would earn them high standings in their class. Already, in his first season at Eton, Eric made no pretense of seeking to place high in his election, or even in the general College standings. Rebels had no need of such things as prestige and rank, and Eric was perceived as a rebel.

Others saw him simply as a lazy young man unwilling to exert himself and put his unquestionably great gifts and talents to work. He lacked discipline, concluded the teachers in whose classes he studied, and even Gow, Eric's tutor, thought that the boy displayed more indolence than independence. There was little doubt that he would manage to survive his career at Eton, but few felt that he would go any farther in his academic career. It seemed unlikely that he would earn entry into any university.

Eric presented a posture of disdain for such criticism. He

had, even at fourteen, few intentions of pursuing an academic career beyond Eton. University scholars and graduates went on to teach at schools such as Eton—or St. Cyprian's if they were of less than first rank—pursuing quiet paths, perhaps teaching at universities themselves. Such paths seemed dull to Eric Blair. He respected scholars such as Gow—as much as he respected anyone in those days—but their lives were too tranquil for him. Eric continued to maintain that he would become a great writer, famous and respected, and that scholars and professors would one day huddle quietly over *his* works.

Although his attitudes toward academic life were rebellious (or lazy) his decision to go no further than Eton was not unusual. For many members of his election, and for most Etonians, the school provided their final formal schooling. Boys from wealthy industrial families left Eton to take their places in the family business; some Etonians entered immediately a career in banking, others distinguished themselves in civil or military service, or in politics; and some indeed became great scholars and outstanding teachers. But for most, Eton was the platform from which a graduate launched himself into a career.

In 1917 the career that many Etonians found immediately facing them was the military. The toll of young men taken by World War I grew larger hourly; hundreds of thousands of young men were dead, many of them led into battle by officers who'd attended Eton. Chapel services each morning included announcements of Etonians killed or wounded in the war, along with a tabulation of the number of graduates and students from the school who served in Europe. By war's end nearly one-fifth of the almost six thousand Etonians who served had been killed, with almost fifteen hundred more wounded.

Some students did not wait for graduation to join the army: they left school, enlisted, and many of them died while still teenagers. Those who remained at Eton came to feel—some of them maintaining that they were *made* to feel—a certain guilt over their avoidance of the battlefield. It was not so bad for

Eric's election: he and his classmates were still too young to serve, but it did strike them occasionally that they might not be aging quickly enough to suit their elders.

Patriotic fervor gripped Britain. Richard Blair, by now sixty years old, enlisted in the army, determined to do his duty despite his age. He did not see combat, but was posted to Marseilles, on the southeastern coast of France, where he helped supply arriving and departing troops. It was not a glamorous position, but Richard Blair was doing his part.

Ida Blair, too, felt the call of patriotism. She shut down the Blair house and moved to London, where she found a secretarial job, working in the government department responsible for pensions. Marjorie also went to London and took a job aiding in the war effort. Such family dedication was common—everyone was eager to do what he or she could for their country and against its enemies. There was a sense in Britain of a nation alive as one being and united by a determination to win the war no matter what the cost in young men's lives.

Among men even younger than the soldiers, though, the rush of patriotism began slowly to change into something different. It was difficult being a bright adolescent during that war: one day nationalistic fever ran high, while the next would be filled with a hatred of uniforms and flags. Nor was military glory so fashionable as it once had been. Eric and his fellows of the election of 1916 began to express increasingly pacifist sentiments. In part their growing opposition to violence was prompted by the more parochial violence aimed at them by the upperclassmen. Eric and others vowed that with their election an end would be brought to the mildly sadistic tormenting of younger students. Also contributing to their growing unwillingness to be captivated by the war and by military institutions was the fact that Eton had made student participation in the Officers' Training Corps (OTC) mandatory. Everyone had to serve, all had to march and drill in uniform, no matter what their personal sentiment.

Compulsory participation in a military training program sat

no better with Eric than did anything compulsory, and he almost immediately began to search for ways of eluding or defeating the regimen required of OTC cadets. He arranged to be placed in the signal section, with its flags, semaphores, and related paraphernalia, and brought to his position a disregard for responsibility that those who served beneath him enjoyed. During field drills with the other students, Eric Blair would, as often as not, find some means of escaping from the exercise, leading his men to secluded spots where they would loosen their uniforms and relax, reading and chatting. Eric, all realized quickly, had no more future as a soldier than he had as a scholar. None of which mattered to Eric: he was going to be a writer.

Eric was not, however, doing a great deal of writing. Certainly, he spent a great deal more time talking about the works he would write than he did practicing literature with pencil and paper. His apathy, or antipathy, toward structure and regimen seemed to extend even to the discipline required to master the art of making sentences. Nor did his studies, and the courses he selected, seem to help prepare him for a literary career. He could not make up his mind what area of study he wanted to concentrate upon, shifting from his declared intent as a classical specialist, to the less stringent requirements of the classical general. Generalists, he believed, were in many ways freed from focusing upon individual elements of literature and were more able to see the larger connections between literature and history. That was just talk, though: the generalist faced less strict requirements than the specialist, and the relaxation permitted Eric more time to pursue his own course of outside reading.

By the time of the summer holidays in 1918 and the end of a full year at Eton, Eric Blair had established a rhythm that suited him, if not his teachers or parents. Although he would occasionally apply himself with some discipline to his classwork or pass through a frenzied few days of writing, he preferred to avoid necessary work and spend his time reading and studying contemporary, rather than classical writers.

H. G. Wells remained one of his favorite novelists, and

Eric, by now fifteen years old, became increasingly aware of the political messages that underlay much of Wells's work. In 1918 Wells was at the height of his fame, having coined the descriptive phrase "the war that will end war" to describe World War I, as well as having written *Mr. Britling Sees it Through*, which was considered to be the great novel of the war years. In this and most of his other works, Wells argued for a revolution in government, an end to nations, an abolition of war, and the formation of a world state. Wells had begun his career more than two decades earlier by writing overtly socialist novels and stories, but by 1918 he was moving beyond socialism in search of his own individual synthesis of government and economics.

For Eric and his classmates of the 1916 election, though, socialism remained attractive, and when queried by Eton as to the most important and influential men still alive, many of the students placed Lenin high on the list. (The Russian Revolution had taken place in 1917.) Such recognition of the Russian revolutionary's influence was honest and accurate, but it was also indicative of the ways in which Eric and his fellow students were changing. They were not the traditional Etonians, or felt they weren't, and as World War I drew toward its close they endeavored to put their differences into action. They had promised to do away with the physical torment of new classes, and when the boys of 1916 achieved seniority they did, indeed, inflict less painful initiations upon the newcomers than their own seniors had inflicted upon them. The revolution, as Eric and others saw it, was short lived, bullying being too institutionalized to be done away with for long.

Socialism, pacifism, fascination with revolutionaries, all were indicative of the changes taking place in the world. The ravages of the war made those changes palpable to young men such as Eric Blair. For all his lack of discipline about the process of writing, Eric remained determined to become a writer, and alert for ways in which the changes moving through society would affect a literary career. H. G. Wells had been one of the first serious writers to exploit science as a literary theme, and in the fall of 1918, perhaps thinking about Wells and his masterful scientific romances, Eric abandoned classics and became a science student, concentrating upon biology. If the diffidence he displayed in classics courses was offset somewhat by his genuine literary interests and gifts, his decision to pursue a scientific education proved an almost total disaster. Eric had no aptitude for mathematics, no talent for understanding fundamental scientific principles and theories. The only real gift he showed was the use of his slingshot for killing birds, which he dissected poorly in class. Eric's flirtation with biology lasted barely a year before he returned to more general studies.

He returned, however, different, his own biology having begun to exact a transformation. During his year in science, as his grades slumped, Eric's height increased. He'd been accustomed to being one of the shortest boys in his election, standing barely five feet four inches at age fifteen. By the summer of 1919 he'd reached five feet seven inches, and was continuing to grow at a rapid rate. His chubbiness changed into thinness. He wondered how tall he would become, and could see himself now as a young man, still in school, but with adulthood and responsibility coming closer daily. His increased sense of maturity led him to flirt poetically with his childhood friend Jacintha Buddicom, but the poems he wrote to her dripped with such overbearing romanticism that Jacintha was more turned off than attracted. She sought courteously to cool Eric's ardor, and although he continued to hunt during holidays with Prosper Buddicom, and to discuss literature with Jacintha, their separate courses were becoming established. After Eric left Eton they lost track of each other for decades.

The failure of his courtship, as he thought of it, left no serious scars. Eric Blair, by the summer of 1920, growing toward six feet even as he descended toward the bottom of the class rankings, was a young man who seemed unaffected by life's disappointments or difficulties, at least in public. He shrugged them off with casual comments and jokes; poor grades and official displeasure were coming to appear almost as goals he sought. Pressed by another mandatory rule at Eton, he allowed himself to be confirmed into the Anglican Church near the end of World War I, with his mother present to witness it. But this was only after he had insulted the teacher who had prepared him and joked loudly about the meaninglessness of religion and religious ceremony. Eric continued to criticize his parents and their beliefs and values, mocking to his friends his father's position as a mulekeeper during the war, spending much of his holiday time with Prosper and Jacintha, avoiding his own home as much as possible. Books carried home for summer lessons often went unopened through the entire season. And at Eton when he should have been studying, he could often be found fishing, lost in thought, a book open on the riverbank beside him. Usually it was a book he was reading for pleasure or personal enlightenment, not for an assignment.

As the new decade approached, Eric began to display an increasing fascination with the lives and conditions of the very poor. In part this awakening of interest was brought on by his reading of Jack London, and especially London's *The People of the Abyss*. First published in 1903, *The People of the Abyss* was London's account of his life among the lowest levels of society in Britain. London's book was filled with great horror and anger, the story of children born into a world with no prospect at all of a better life, of parents who fought in the mud over scraps of food found among garbage, of squalor, of dirt, of odor, of helplessness and hopelessness. Jack London was a powerful writer who made the social forces that condemned people to this abyss come as alive for the reader as he did the forces of nature in books such as *The Call of the Wild* and *White Fang*. And just as in those books London wrote of individual strength and willpower being necessary to combat natural forces, in *The People of the Abyss* and his novel *The Iron Heel* he wrote of the need for great strength and a willingness to commit, if not embrace, violence in order to triumph over poverty and an unjust social order.

Eric responded emotionally to London's works, fascinated by this writer who had lived among the poor in order to write truly about them. Despite Eric's own feelings of insecurity about his family background—he could not forget how he'd felt when he learned that he attended St. Cyprian's on scholarship—he knew how privileged his own life had been. He had never been hungry as the poor were hungry, never cold as they were cold, never smelled so bad as they did. Yet, even as he was awakening to the plight of the poor, in fact, he spoke harshly of their unpleasant odor, as though to him it were a racial characteristic rather than the result of poor hygiene.

In late summer of 1920, Eric had the opportunity to indulge in a bit of journeying among the poor himself. He'd been in London, in his Officers' Training Corps uniform and cape, when he missed the train to Looe, in Cornwall, where his family was vacationing. He found himself stranded in a small village station, Seaton Junction. He sent a telegram to inform his parents of the delay and caught a train to Plymouth, where he hoped to make the connection that would carry him on to Cornwall, and his parents.

Arriving in Plymouth, though, he discovered that he'd missed his connection and that another train would not arrive until morning. It was too late for another telegram, and his funds were limited. Eric had enough money to eat or to secure a bed at the Plymouth YMCA, but not enough to do both. It was late afternoon and the demands of his stomach overrode his desire for a warm bed, so he spent his money on sweet rolls, then set about searching for a place to spend the night. He would have to sleep outdoors, exposed to the chilly English evening weather, and looked for a likely spot. As he walked, Eric was pleased to notice that the few people he passed evidently took him for a soldier, asking if he had been demobilized along with others who'd returned from the war in Europe. He was less pleased by a recurrent thought: the punishment for sleeping outdoors, with no visible means of income, was two weeks in jail. He forced himself to be very cautious, moving slowly through a farmer's field, growing frightened when it seemed that any movement he made awakened the neighborhood dogs whose barking, Eric was certain, would alert the police.

At last he found a spot beneath a tree, but his uniform and cape did little to keep him warm. He tossed and turned fitfully for most of the night, finally falling asleep in the small hours only to sleep so soundly that he missed the first train to Cornwall. He caught the second, though, arrived in Looe, and after a four-mile walk was reunited with his family. He immediately set to writing letters to his classmates in which he told them in great detail of his adventures as a tramp surviving by wit alone, like the boys in *The Coral Island,* Ballantyne's book that Eric had loved so much.

Not long after his night in the field, Eric returned to Eton for his final year. Only one member of the election of 1916 stood lower in the ranks than Eric Blair. In the fall of 1920 Eric concentrated upon history as his major, but by the beginning of 1921 he had returned to classics. Eric now stood more than six feet tall with a slouch that matched his cynical outlook. He indulged in an occasional cigarette, strictly forbidden at Eton, and when he was once caught with an empty cigarette pack he openly showed his contempt for Eton's rules and those who sought to enforce them. Eric argued with those who lectured him, meeting their scoldings with his own scorn. His time at Eton was drawing to a close, and he felt increasingly free to speak his mind.

There was a brief flirtation with the thought of going on to Oxford, the impetus for the flirtation coming primarily from Jacintha Buddicom. As a King's Scholar at Eton, Eric could have won entry to Oxford, but because of his grades would not have been eligible for a scholarship. Without the scholarship, his father pointed out, there was no question of Eric's attending a university: the tuition was more than the family could bear. Besides, with an Eton education, Eric would be able to make his own way in the world, and at age eighteen it was time that he should begin to do so. As the spring of 1921 began to bloom, Eric began to cast about for a career.

He was already half decided. He did not feel himself ready to support himself as a writer, and since he would have to find a job, he wanted one likely to provide him with the materials out of which literature could be fashioned. He recalled his father's stories of life in India, he had read and reread Kipling's tales and poems of colonial life, and Ida Blair's mother still lived in Moulmein, Burma. The colonial service appealed to Eric, and he began to look at the requirements for finding a position in India.

There were not many options open to him. The more prestigious posts required a university education. Eric Blair found himself eligible for positions in the colonial police, the Forestry or Roads Departments, as an official serving the Public Health Department, or even as an officer in his father's old service, the Opium Department. The opium controversy had continued to grow, however, and by 1921 the department was nearing the end of its existence. Forests, roads, and public health held no appeal for Eric, but the Imperial Indian Police sounded as though it might be exciting, although he was amused by the irony of his choice. By the end of the summer he had essentially made up his mind, and he entered his final season at Eton more uninterested than ever.

In December 1921, Eric Blair left Eton for the last time. His last term had passed uneventfully, with the exception of his sole athletic triumph: the scoring of a difficult goal during an important game. There were no academic triumphs.

Eric spent the Christmas holidays with his parents in their new home in Southwold, a small resort town on the coast. Although school was behind him, study was not, for in January 1922, Eric undertook six months of hard tutoring that would prepare him for the Indian Police's entrance examinations. The examinations lasted a week, covering the applicants' knowledge of mathematics, history, English, and French, all of which were required. As his elective examination topics, Eric was tested in his ability to draw, as well as in his mastery of Latin and Greek. Aware that this time a career, and not simply academic standing, was at stake, Eric applied himself diligently, studying hard, no matter how irrelevant the subjects seemed. He was rewarded by placing seventh out of the top twenty-six applicants. That position would be lowered considerably as a result of the poor horsemanship he displayed during the compulsory riding examination, but he'd still done well enough to win a posting.

He was awarded the rank of probationary assistant superintendent of police as soon as he was nineteen, the minimum age for admission into the service. Eric requested assignment to Burma, where he had relatives. As Burma was not one of the more desirable destinations for young men in search of adventure and advancement, his request was granted. He received his orders and would sail in October.

Eric Blair, about to embark upon a career in the civil service, possessed of literary ambitions but with little prospect of making those ambitions a reality, spent the late summer months packing his belongings. He listened dutifully to his father as Richard Blair offered advice based upon experience gained during a life in the colonies. He promised to visit his grandmother in Moulmein.

He passed what free time he had reading, fishing, and talking. He visited Jacintha and Prosper, and made clear that his literary goals still existed, that he was postponing his career, not abandoning it. He'd not written a great deal at Eton. There were his love poems to Jacintha, moral stories and fables for his instructors, pieces for occasional Eton publications, but he showed no signs of being a prodigy. If he was going to become a writer, a good deal of work lay ahead of him.

If Eric Blair had not made his mark on Eton, the school at least had left its ineradicable mark upon him. Despite the disdain he'd been so eager to show, Eric was very much the proper young Etonian. The school's influence and attitudes were obvious in his demeanor, in his outlook, his sense that he was equal to the challenges that lay ahead of him.

On October 27, 1922, Probationary Assistant Superintendent of Police Eric Blair boarded the SS *Herefordshire*, bound for Rangoon, and from Rangoon for posting as policeman in Burma.

FOUR

BLAIR IN BURMA

THE VOYAGE ITSELF WAS a revelation. Blair passed long hours at the rail, watching the wake cast by the *Herefordshire* as it bore him toward the East. Even as the ship left England, Blair was beginning deliberately to postpone his plans for becoming a writer. One of the attractions of the Imperial Police was its promise of retirement with a pension at forty. Forty, thought Blair, was young enough to undertake a writing career; the pension would make his support easier until his works began to sell.

He could in a fit of self-pity or self-indulgence dream of deferring his literary ambitions, but he could not disengage the qualities a good writer most needs: attentiveness to language, awareness of detail, acuteness of observation. Blair stood by the rail of the ship and watched Britain recede, then turned his attention to his fellow passengers and the crew that served them. The crew was predominantly Indian, but the officers were British, and there were several Europeans among the crew. It was they who handled any mechanical emergency that might arise. Blair was fascinated by these men, awed by their array of skills. But his feeling was tempered when he spotted one of them, after the midday meal, smuggling leftover food from the galley back to his quarters, a guilty look on his face. Blair was never to forget that glimpse of a man he'd admired, a skilled man, reduced to becoming a petty thief in order to feed himself.

When the *Herefordshire* made landfall in Colombo, Sri Lanka (or Ceylon, as it was then known), Blair's eyes were again opened. The ship became crowded with Sri Lankans who scurried up the gangplanks in search of work, most of which consisted of helping passengers with their luggage. The coolies, as they were called, were under the supervision of the local white police, Blair's own colleagues, and Blair watched as the coolies were prodded to work harder and were brutally kicked when they became clumsy. Was this the sort of duty for which he was to be responsible? It did not escape his notice that the white passengers complimented the policemen for well-aimed, well-timed kicks.

By November Blair had landed in Rangoon, and his concern for coolies was replaced by the exotic distractions of the place. He was struck by the golden spires of Buddhist shrines, and by the contrast of the stacks and towers of the Rangoon oil refinery, which reached equally high but spat smoke rather than reflecting sunlight. Ancient, exotic, modern, Eastern, Western, Rangoon's cultures mingled in a throbbing, noisy throng, almost overwhelming at first, with a fevered rhythm that took some getting used to. Blair, as was expected of him, introduced himself to the local colonial officials, and after a few days found himself growing more relaxed in India. Soon he caught the train that would carry him to Mandalay and the school at which he would be instructed in the art and science of becoming a colonial police officer. The train trip lasted sixteen hours, carrying Blair far north and into central Burma, to Mandalay on the Irrawaddy River.

Mandalay, celebrated in one of Kipling's poems, dominated by a nearly one-mile-square fortified palace surrounded by a moat thick with hyacinths, struck Blair at first as a city as marvelously exotic as Rangoon. And there was no odorous refinery to foul the air in Mandalay. For all their exotic nature, however, neither city was ancient. Rangoon had been founded by King Alaungpaya in 1755, and Mandalay by King Mindon barely a century later in 1857. The streets of Rangoon had been planned by British engineers, and Mindon had copied that layout. Mandalay was to be the capital of Burma. It was built around the central palace and the Buddhist Shwe Nandaw Monastery, but in 1885 British troops captured the city, overthrew Mindon's successor, and proclaimed Rangoon the country's capital. Mandalay became an admittedly important colonial outpost, the palace transformed into a British fort, the city a central location from which control of the region could be exercised.

Imperial influence extended far beyond the layout of city streets. In fact, in 1922, even with the number of British troops declining, it extended beyond mere influence. It pervaded Burmese society, seeking to overwhelm any national identity and replace it with a more subservient colonial identity. The British Empire during the 1920s remained an *empire*, in which the crown's absolute authority was enforced by troops if necessary, but more often by colonial police and administrative officials. During the 1920s, though, both Indian and Burmese independence movements were beginning to grow, India's more rapidly and forcefully than that of Burma. Burma was viewed by the British as an Indian province, and those imperial concessions that were made to the independence movements favored India far more than they did Burma.

Provincial administration, especially in outlying and underdeveloped areas, fell largely to the provincial police that Eric Blair had joined. The policemen were often either Burmese or Indian—although there were more than a few Chinese among the ranks—and these were supervised by white officers. The challenges facing the provincial police grew apace with the spread of fervor for independence, and to meet these challenges a lengthy training period was required of new officers. For nine months Blair and his fellow new arrivals were billeted at the police mess in Mandalay as they undertook their course of study.

For the new officers that curriculum included both the Burmese language and the Indian Hindustani language, which was also spoken in Burma. Officers were expected to become fluent in both languages, along with local dialects, and to understand more technical legal terms and conversation in both languages. They were responsible for courses in police methods and procedure, as well as local and British administrative law. In addition, they learned the various means and methods of controlling their subordinates.

On Wednesdays and Saturdays the probationary officers were expected to attend full-dress parades of those subordinates. More than one hundred of the Indian, Burmese, and Chinese cadets were attending the Police School in Mandalay during Blair's term there, and the parades were an important part of each week. The probationary officers were required to wear their formal dress uniforms to the parades, looking like something out of Kipling: British officers in white with sabers, reviewing the natives. While it made a very dashing picture, Blair never quite managed to present the striking colonial officer image of his colleagues. He'd grown quite tall but also quite skinny, the chubbiness of his youth now long gone. Blair's uniforms tended to hang loosely on him, no matter how tightly they were recut and tailored.

During his training period in Burma Blair lived in quarters his father would have well understood. The police mess was a comfortable large building whose ground floor served the white officers as their club. It was to the club that many officers retired for drinks, conversation, and cards at the end of the day, just as they had during Richard Blair's years with the Opium Department. But if the details of club life—and clubmen, as they thought of themselves—had changed little since the reign of Queen Victoria, the cost of the club had gone up precipitously. Eric Blair, at least, could afford only occasional visits, having to spend most of his meager salary on the simple business of keeping alive.

His inability to join in the more social aspects of an officer's life mattered little to Blair. His shyness, always pronounced, grew deeper during his days in Burma. He did not like meeting new people, he had no gift for small talk or idle chatter. He did not particularly enjoy the topics of conversation practiced in the club, either. His fellow officers seemed to spend all their time speaking of women, or of the inferiority of the dark-skinned peoples with whom they were surrounded, or of their experiences in combat during World War I. The older officers rarely overlooked the opportunity to make Blair and others his age feel inadequate for having been too young to take part in the war.

Blair preferred to spend his free time in his room, reading. He'd brought with him a number of books, novels, primarily, and other English-language publications were easily available. As the courses required of the probationary officers, particularly their language courses, were left to a certain degree to the individual student's initiative and ability, Blair often was able to spend whole days in his room reading. He studied on his own and remained ahead of his classmates in most of the studies, his gift for languages enabling him to excel in his mastery of Burmese and Hindustani. Blair deliberately created the impression of wishing to be left alone, and his wishes were for the most part respected.

When he was not reading or studying, Blair prowled about Mandalay, learning as much as he could on his own of the nature of the country to which he'd requested assignment. Local history and culture were given short shrift at the Police School, being seen as unimportant to colonial administrators. Blair sought to remedy that lack on his own. After he'd been in Mandalay several weeks he managed to save enough money to buy a second-hand motorcycle. His classmates were amused by the picture of Blair on the bike. It fit him no better than did his uniforms, his knees coming, it seemed, all the way up to his oversized ears as he hunched over the handlebars.

The topic of women, so popular among the officers, was one that caused Blair some discomfort. He was not at ease around women, and with the exception of his poetic attempt at the courtship of Jacintha Buddicom, along with one or two other minor crushes, he had yet to experience a serious romantic attachment. He was too shy. Blair managed to overcome that shyness on occasion, however, and indulge in a bit of bragging about his amorous adventures among Mandalay's bordellos, but whether or not his tales were based upon fact was unknown. He did seem to display less interest in female companionship than did other young men his age.

From time to time he was willing to engage in adventures of other sorts. While stationed in Mandalay he and a friend decided that their assignment would be incomplete without a tiger hunt, and they planned the undertaking with care. When they received some time off from their studies they traveled along muddy roads deep into the jungle to meet a guide they had hired. The guide then loaded them into a wooden cart drawn by a bull, and led them ever deeper into the jungle. He was leading them, they were assured, to a spot where they would encounter a fierce, trophy-sized tiger. They rode all night, the guide offered constant encouragement, but they saw no tigers. It was only as they made their way back to the police mess that Blair and his companion became convinced that the guide, perhaps resentful of British officers, had led them only to spots where no tiger was likely to be found.

Such companionship in adventure was uncommon for Blair, however, and he accomplished most of his explorations on his own. As the weeks of his training passed he retreated more and more into himself. He wrote few letters. At first, as though still convinced that a romance could be kindled, he wrote to Jacintha Buddicom, complaining of how awful he found everything, of how much he disliked the country. Jacintha was no more receptive to his complaints than she'd been to his plaintive declarations of romance. She responded with practical advice, telling Blair to grow accustomed to his surroundings or to abandon the service and return home. Eric wrote three letters to Jacintha, but either her responses were not what he wished to hear, or he lost interest in writing of complaints, for their correspondence dwindled and then ceased altogether.

He did little writing of any sort while in Burma. Occasionally he would sit with pen and huddle over a piece of paper—often official stationery purloined for a literary purpose—and after much effort produce a poem. It was becoming clear to Blair, though, that his talents, whatever they were, were not wholly poetic. His Burmese poetry seemed little better than his schoolboy verse, and in all his years in Burma he wrote fewer than half-a-dozen poems. Was the dream of becoming a writer, delayed and deferred, in the process of being denied by Blair?

Certainly there were plenty of activities to keep him busy. In January 1924 he graduated from the Police School and received his first assignment. He remained a probationary officer, as regulations dictated, and would hold that position for another fifteen months. But his first posting, to Myaungmya in the south, where the Irrawaddy broadened as it made its way to the ocean, carried with it a great deal of responsibility. Under the supervision of an embittered, demanding superior officer, Blair was held accountable for a variety of tasks, including the direction of more than three dozen local policemen, and the accuracy and promptness with which all local records were kept. He was also responsible for the management and maintenance of the local version of the police school, as well as teaching native candidates who were studying to be police officers. His superior was frequently absent and Blair more than once found himself in absolute command of the Myaungmya police station with its attendant courts, school, and responsibilities.

The posting lasted barely a season. Blair was transferred to Twante in late spring, 1924. Twante was smaller than Myaungmya, and Blair carried even more authority in his new posting. In Twante he lived in a house that lacked all of the amenities to which Europeans were accustomed: there was no running water, toilets, or electricity. Blair was rarely at home, however, taking his motorcycle out for patrols through the area, checking on legal matters in villages even smaller than Twante, serving as a magistrate, and supervising the Burmese policemen. Although Twante was less than twenty miles by canal from Rangoon, Blair saw few other Europeans during his stay there. His superiors would occasionally visit, if only to insure that he was doing all right. Blair continued to keep his own counsel, seeking to be fair in the justice he delivered, while he learned the role of colonial police officer.

His performance was not distinguished, but neither was it incompetent. Blair set a steady course for himself, quiet, solitary, neither overeager nor lackadaisical. He was an ordinary, bookish sort of fellow who made few close friends and who earned some attention for his regular attendance at native churches—both Christian and Buddhist. As an assistant district superintendent, albeit probationary, he accepted his duties and spent most of his time carrying them out.

While those duties primarily involved the exercise of civil law and the supervision of police forces, there were occasional murders to which Blair was assigned as an investigator. This, at first, was more like the police work he recalled from the books he read as a boy. There was a sense of excitement that came with riding in a canoe paddled by Burmese, Blair in his uniform bringing authority and order, to small villages where a crime had been committed. He almost enjoyed it. It was almost possible, while seeking evidence or gathering testimony in a capital crime, to feel some of the romance he'd imagined he would find in Burma. And it was almost possible, once the investigation and trial ended, to watch the execution by hanging of the criminal and imagine that, in some way, justice had been done. But was justice served by a criminal's death, by any death? Blair did not know.

Murder cases in the Twante area, however, were relatively rare, and their nature was usually that of a crime of quick flaring passion rather than careful calculation, as in detective stories. More common than murderers, and more problematical to deal with, were the gangs of thieves who roved through the area, attacking and robbing villages and travelers alike. Thievery was endemic in outlying regions, and some of the bands of thieves grew quite large and vicious, eluding the best efforts of Blair and his police force.

He came to enjoy working with the Burmese, but it was not a rapid process. The empire had been a fact for all of his life, and its nature—and the right of its existence—had been reinforced by his education both at St. Cyprian's and Eton. The British had carried their culture and knowledge to this part of the world, and would make the Burmese accept it, by force when required. And, despite the decline in the number of troops stationed in Burma, force was still frequently required.

The British rarely identified Asians by any term other than a derogatory one. Discipline was accomplished by cursing them, and if this failed the British felt free to strike the Burmese. Eric Blair, still uncertain of himself, barely twenty-one years old, carried a cane on occasion. If he did not become a sadistic tormentor of the Burmese as did so many of the British, he could still grow sufficiently annoyed, often over very minor slights, to wield the cane, as Mr. Wilkes had done at St. Cyprian's. He struck some harsh blows with it, he made some points with it, and never revealed whether he'd forgotten the effort of his Eton election to abolish violence.

Times were changing in Burma, though, and on one occasion Blair used his cane to strike a Burmese student who had inadvertently jostled him. To his surprise, Blair found himself immediately surrounded by angry students. Their education might be a product of the British presence, but its results were prodding them to resist the right of the white man to inflict casual, painful blows. Burmese students understood that a day was coming when the British would no longer be granted the rights they had claimed for more than a century: the right to exploit the land until it was exhausted, the right to mine its resources and carry the profits home with them, the right to use, and often kill, the Burmese people by simple virtue of military and economic superiority and white skins. There were consequences to be paid for such actions.

Typically for Blair, the confrontation with the students avoided further violence, devolving into a shouted debate as both Blair and the students sought to make their points. The argument continued for some time, the students following Blair onto a train. Despite the heat of the moment, both Blair and the students seemed more interested ultimately in ideas than in physical confrontation. Blair was not certain he disagreed with the students.

By early 1925 Blair had been transferred to his third posting, this one at Syriam, even closer to Rangoon than was Twante. Syriam was a refinery town, its air acrid with smoke, its ground so fouled by industrial by-products that it was virtually unable to support vegetation. Syriam was a rough spot as well, with Burmese refinery workers who sometimes seemed to look upon their labor as an interlude between bouts of drinking and fighting. There was a murder virtually every day, but Blair's primary responsibilities lay not in murder investigation, but in helping supervise security for the refinery and going on long patrols to outlying villages. There was no variety in the work, and few challenges; police work in Syriam soon came to strike Blair as being nearly as stultifying as the foul fumes that ruined the air.

He continued to devote his free time to reading, concentrating on novels. Despite his distance both geographically and professionally from the British literary scene, Blair attempted to keep up to date with the works of important contemporary writers. He would go on jags, reading one novel after another by D. H. Lawrence, for example, or passing hours with an acquaintance discussing the works of Aldous Huxley, an up-and-coming novelist. Blair recalled Huxley as a substitute French instructor at Eton, and was able to add his memories of Huxley's personality to his discussions of Huxley's work.

Another English writer Blair admired and turned to often was W. Somerset Maugham. Novels such as *Of Human Bondage,* and Maugham's many short stories, struck Blair as models of clear, straightforward storytelling. He appreciated Maugham's "plain" style. For its time, it was a relaxed and unmannered style of writing that erected few barriers of allusion or metaphor between writer and reader. Maugham had seen and written about the Far East, and Blair also found that agreeable.

In addition to his attempts at staying current with English literature, Blair was reading the works of an earlier generation. He particularly enjoyed Mark Twain, and could lose himself in the works of Tolstoy. Joseph Conrad's novels and the short stories of Edgar Allan Poe also caught Blair's interest. He read avidly the works of Samuel Butler, the nineteenth-century English novelist and essayist. Butler had written *Erewhon,* a satirical novel of a world in which possession of machines was illegal. Blair appreciated Butler's use of fantasy as a means of making intellectual points. He also studied Butler's *Notebooks,* which were filled with practical comments about writing.

There were few people with whom Blair could discuss his literary interests, and no one to whom he divulged his literary ambitions. He would claim later that those ambitions had been put out of his mind when he put on the uniform of the provincial police. Most of his fellow officers, especially the older ones, expressed attitudes verging on contempt toward novels, novelists, and intellectuals in general. They thought of themselves as hard practical men, tough men whose job it was to hold the empire together, or at least their own particular corner of it. If they had a favorite writer, it was Kipling, who had seen what they had seen, knew what they knew, and had written it down for the world. Even Blair admitted that part of his attraction to service in the police in Burma was derived from his reading of Kipling.

As his years in Burma passed, though, Blair's affection for Kipling began to wane, as *he* saw what Kipling had seen, and came to know the modern version of the world Kipling had known. During his first two years in Burma, though, and through his first few postings, Blair was very much a part of that

Kiplingesque world. For all that his uniforms did not fit him well, he wore them proudly, taking great pleasure in the way a uniform made a man feel. And despite his predilection for lingering in his room over a book, he could occasionally be found in the local club, smoking a cigarette and having a drink with his colleagues, discussing with them the day's work.

His pleasure in that vision of himself began to fade as more time passed. The climate of Burma—and no doubt the cigarettes that he had taken to smoking constantly—did not agree with his lungs. He experienced occasional bouts with congestion and bronchial trouble. During the monsoon seasons his health would sink to its lowest point, and his early postings that carried him south into the Irrawaddy Delta also took him to the area of Burma where the monsoons were most severe.

Nor did he have a great deal of luck with his superior officers. While he was taken with the idea of colonial service, and pleased with the feel of his uniform with its straps and buckles, Eric Blair was by no means a conventional young colonial officer. He was too open, too receptive, and as the years passed it became obvious that he was too empathetic toward the Burmese over whom he was supposed to exercise authority. Blair had servants, as did all the other officers, but when those officers would visit Blair's quarters they would often find him living in a tumbledown hut, with a variety of animals that he'd adopted running loose through his bedroom. Servants, the others pointed out, were supposed to deal with messes like that. But, Blair responded, the mess was the way he enjoyed living. The officer's mold that he had tried to fit was beginning to crack.

By the end of the summer of 1925, Blair had been transferred out of the Delta and back into jungle country, to Insein, ten miles to the north of Rangoon. It was at his new posting that Blair began to entertain his first serious doubts about the service in which he had enlisted. His growing dissatisfaction could be traced partly to the passage of time: nothing about Burma was new to him any longer, he had seen it all and the days and chores became repetitive and depressing. Blair was too imaginative: Insein was the site of a major Burmese prison, with thousands of Burmese incarcerated there, many of them awaiting execution. Their captive presence was a constant reminder to officers such as Blair of the authority they held over other's lives. Blair's superior in Insein made his own contributions to the young officer's disappointment with the service. The superior officer possessed a reputation for tormenting his juniors that was by every evidence well earned. To be trapped in a dull job, in proximity to thousands of men waiting to die, and hounded by a superior without sympathy or concern, was more than Blair could stand. He began to speak of leaving the police.

His stay in Insein lasted an endless six months, each day weighing more heavily upon Blair than the previous one. By April 1926, when he was transferred to Moulmein, his decision to leave Burma was virtually complete. Certainly his early determination to become a model police officer was gone. Even the distractions of being posted in a large city, the home of his maternal grandmother, could not spark in him a renewal of interest. He told his grandmother, in fact, that he was giving thought to the best way of leaving the service. He found her unsympathetic. The Limouzin family had settled in Burma generations before and bore the obligations of colonials as comfortably as anyone. On a more pragmatic level, Mrs. Limouzin was curious as to what her grandson would do after leaving the service. He had no answer.

It became more and more clear to him, though, that departure from Burma and abandonment of his police career were inevitable. He was not meant for this way of life. His argument with the students over his right to strike them made a good example of what was wrong. Blair, the white man, the British officer, was granted by virtue of the circumstances of his birth the right to strike blows against other human beings. Yet when the argument continued on board the train, those supposedly lesser humans rode with him in the same car, their first-class tickets as good as his own. Their eyes, for that matter, were as alive with the student's love of learning as, at one time, his had been. What right did he have to strike them?

He grew more aware of the hatred that lay beneath the surface servility of the Burmese. And why should they not hate the British, the Europeans, and the Americans who destroyed their land and their hopes? The question of authority began to obsess him. Blair, as a young officer, was occasionally presented with tasks that were intended to reinforce that authority. But whether he was called upon to help in a criminal investigation, witness a hanging, or shoot an elephant that had gone mad, Blair no longer saw the respect for uniform and empire in Burmese eyes that he'd seen upon first arriving in Burma. Now he saw more deeply and could see or sense the laughter, contemptuous and disrespectful, that lurked behind those eyes. It would erupt one day, he began to realize, and the eruption would most likely be violent, perhaps terribly so. The empire had outlived its usefulness, or at least Eric Blair felt he had outlived his own usefulness to the empire.

Eric Blair received what would be his final posting during the Christmas holidays in 1926. He was transferred to Katha, far to the north of Mandalay, in a more temperate region of Burma. The change in climate helped his health little. His cough was chronic now, and he suspected more than once that he had tuberculosis. As the early months of 1927 passed he began to think of his health as a legitimate excuse for leaving the service. Late in 1927 he would complete his first five years of Burmese duty, and would be eligible for a long leave of absence. Perhaps during the leave he could renew his discipline if not his dedication, and return to Burma refreshed.

That brief hope faded quickly. By June he knew that he could no longer function as a police officer. He put in for a medical leave, not wishing to resign while still in Burma. He could not wait even four months for his regular leave to come up. In July he was granted a medical leave that was to last nearly half a year.

Blair did not hesitate. He packed his bags, said what few

farewells he felt obliged to say, and boarded ship for his return voyage to Britain. Despite his request for a temporary medical leave, he knew that he would not be returning to Burma. He passed his time on board the ship reading, smoking, and thinking about his future. That future, he came to realize with increasing clarity, was one in which he would make of himself a writer. But how to write? And what to write about? As at so many other points in his life, Eric Blair was uncertain.

FIVE

DOWN, OUT,
AND ON THE WAY UP

IN AUGUST 1927, twenty-four-year-old Eric Blair stood on British soil for the first time in five years. In many ways he'd still been a schoolboy when he departed for exotic adventure in Burma, and he was in many ways a man now that he had returned. While overseas, he'd grown a mustache and become a nonstop cigarette smoker, a would-be writer, an adult responsible for his own actions and their consequences. That sense of responsibility, coupled with Blair's belief, as yet unsupported, that he could best meet his responsibilities through the practice of literature, was what he most wanted to communicate to his parents. It would not be easy.

Blair joined his family immediately upon his return from Burma, and traveled with them for a family vacation in Cornwall. For his first few days home he kept quiet not only about his decision to leave the police, but also about the medical leave he'd been granted. The sea voyage had restored him to better health, and despite a brief relapse during which he lay in bed and was cared for by Ida Blair, Blair's health remained generally good and continued to improve.

The same could not be said of his relationship with his parents. Once he was recovered, he steeled himself to reveal his decision. He would not be returning to Burma. More than that, he intended to become a writer, and had decided to seek no

77

professional or salaried position. His frugality in Burma had left him with a few months' pay, enough to get by on until his work was selling regularly.

Richard and Ida Blair had no idea what sort of response to make. They did reveal their displeasure and disappointment, but their son, though it was obvious he cared for their feelings, was not about to change his mind or revise his plans simply to suit them. He'd already drafted his letter of resignation, and mailed it to his superiors in London. Questions about duty, obligation, or, more pragmatically, subsistence, fell upon deaf ears. Blair had seen the empire at work, and learned that it was not his lot to play a part in it. He could make such a decision, he argued, because he had, at least, given the service a chance. He was not his father, who after all the years in the Opium Department had still felt strongly enough to volunteer for service during the war. That was admirable, certainly, but it was not for Eric Blair. He was going to write: it was as simple as that. And he made his points smoking, scattering ashes, tossing half-finished cigarettes on the floor, just as he threw his clothes onto chairs and left stacks of books piled precariously. He gave little evidence of caring for domestic order any more than he did for professional discipline.

The Blairs were baffled and convinced that their son's ambitions would come to nothing. But they were also, despite the now-faded contempt Eric had expressed toward them while at Eton, intelligent and understanding people. They knew there was nothing they could do to change his mind. They made their disappointment clear, and in some ways it never dwindled. But Eric Blair was after all an adult. The path his life was to take was his to decide, so long as he understood that he would have to make his own way. He should not plan to learn to write while depending upon Richard and Ida Blair for support and sustenance. He would visit them occasionally, but they would never again be close. Blair was no longer a child.

Blair had anticipated that attitude, and knew that it was

reasonable. He also knew how great a struggle lay ahead of him, how difficult it was to earn an entry into the world of literature, how much he had to learn, and how little he knew. There were sacrifices to be made, among them, at least temporarily, the respect of his parents. But he was willing to make that sacrifice and whatever others were required, in order to win the success that he felt awaited him. He would one day be able to show Jacintha Buddicom that "collected edition" of which they'd so often spoken as children.

His parents informed of his decision, the police notified of his intention to resign, Blair passed most of a month attempting to get his bearings. He'd chosen his course before he quite knew the best way of proceeding along it. He visited Prosper Buddicom, but Jacintha was away and he could not benefit from her counsel. He traveled back to Eton and spent a brief time with A. S. F. Gow, his first and favorite tutor. Gow gave what encouragement he felt he could, but had little to offer. Other than to recommend that a would-be writer actually spend time *writing*, and then submitting the completed work, there is very little good advice that can be given to a person possessed of literary ambition.

That was all that Eric Blair needed. By fall he had contacted a friend in London and through her had located and rented a small, sparsely furnished room in which to set up his typewriter and begin transforming himself from unemployed former colonial policeman into a self-supporting, consistently published writer. He planned to keep to himself. Blair did not have a great deal of interest in talking about the works he planned, despite the fact that most of his neighbors were writers and artists of various sorts and levels of success. Ruth Pitter, the friend who had found him the room, was herself a published poet, although she did not earn her livelihood from poetry. She was the one person to whom Blair was willing to show his work. He understood that he faced a long apprenticeship, and that idle conversation could too easily take the place of production of completed manuscripts. He plunged into his work, spending most of each day, as well as a good portion of his evening hours, at his typewriter. There was no going back now.

Nor was there, so far as his early pieces were concerned, much looking back, either. Despite the presence on his desk of a large stack of police stationery, purloined in Burma against lean days ahead, Blair seems to have avoided the attempt to deal with his colonial experiences in his early stories and poems. Few of those manuscripts survived, but most of his effort during his first season as a full-time writer was devoted to producing commercial stories, plays, and poems, pieces of work tailored to suit the literary marketplace as Blair viewed it. Burma would one day no doubt be transmuted into books, essays, poems, and short stories, but fall 1927 was too soon to attempt it. Burma and its people were too different, the Burmese experience too complex, his own attitudes toward empire still too chaotic and undefined to allow the production of the careful, good work he set as his goal. Burma also must have seemed less salable as source material for stories than did more literary themes.

As the fall turned into a cold winter and 1928 drew closer, Blair typed out his own versions of the sorts of stories he found most frequently in popular magazines. He wrote of young people, he wrote love stories, he wrote poetry, he endeavored to write a play about a struggling artist whose starving child needed an operation. The play was no more melodramatic and florid than the rest of his early works. Ruth Pitter listened attentively as Blair read some of his attempts to her, and she tactfully waited until the earnest young author had left the room before she burst out laughing. It was not just that he was unskilled; it was as though Blair's brain generated plots, characters, and language that were deliberately overwrought. It struck some of those who were exposed to his apprentice work that he was worse than an amateur; he was a *hopeless* amateur who had no chance of ever becoming a published writer, much less an important one.

If Blair was aware of the others' feelings, it did not deter him. Criticism and rejection could not stop him. He became increasingly withdrawn, the typewriter and blank pages the focal points of his existence. His situation must at times have seemed almost as melodramatic as those he devised for his poor characters. The room he rented was unheated, and as bitter winter settled in, Blair claimed to use a single candle as a means of warming his fingers until they were limber enough to let him work the keys of his typewriter. Blair could not be kept from the typewriter by the elements any more than he could by lack of talent, or parental displeasure, or a constant sense of failure. He swung between that sense of failure and a quiet optimism about his work. He kept on working, in either mood, dedicated to nothing less than mastering the English language. He had to learn how to create sentences, to write clearly, to overcome the handicaps of an overliterary, affected style. He gave the impression of being certain that by mastering language he would have the tool he needed to untangle the knot of emotion and half-formed opinion that kept his writing from being first rate. He knew he had things to say but did not quite know how to say them.

Those emotions and opinions increasingly gathered around the plight of the poor. Blair was not yet ready to undertake serious writing about the oppression he had witnessed, and participated in while stationed in Burma, but he grew more and more aware that there was oppression to be found outside his London room. As his resources dwindled, and his prospects for earning income by his typewriter grew no better, he became curious, and then fascinated with the lives of those who had no prospects at all. The Depression of the 1930s was already beginning to set in even in the late 1920s. Blair was increasingly drawn not only to thought about the poor, to contemplation of their situation and reflection about its nature, but also to physical proximity to poverty. He had to be there, in the poor quarters of London, he had to walk among the poor, and he felt with more and more certainty that he had to do even more than that. He had to walk *as* one of the poor, become one of them.

The early months of 1928 passed and Blair began to put aside his carefully, if poorly crafted commercial stories. He replaced them with fragments, bits of conversation overheard while stalking through poor sections of the city, sketches of the people he saw, and the incidents he witnessed. Blair returned to those places again and again, dressed as a tramp, drawn there by something he still could not articulate, could not make completely clear to himself, much less put down on paper. But the fascination became an obsession, and along with it was something like a conviction that he would find a source for great writing in the stricken lives and the deaths of the poor.

That winter Blair walked London's shabbiest streets, refusing to wear warm clothes because those he watched had none. His lungs began to act up and give him a chronic cough like that of the poverty-seized tubercular people he passed. But Blair began to come alive. To understand the poor he was going to have to live among them, not simply make forays from his artist's quarters, to which he could return whenever he chose. He would have to change lodgings, moving from a clean, cold room to a foul and filthy one. It was a decision made easier by the fact that his savings had dwindled, but there was more to it than practical considerations. There was about him in 1928 something of the scientist going to work in the field while making observations. Blair now saw destitute Londoners differently from the way he'd viewed them in the past, but he remained an educated man who made his expeditions in disguise. There was something of the feeling he'd enjoyed when he missed the vacation train from school: he was living by his wits, as had the heroes of the books of R. M. Ballantyne and others.

There was also in Blair a growing political awareness; more and more of his thoughts took political turns as he learned more about the poor. He could feel an emotional thrill, and a political one, when a rough character, by middle-class standards, caught a glimpse of Eric Blair in theadbare 'clothes, perhaps hunched over a cheap meal, and called him "mate." He was becoming a part of a community whose existence was as solid, and whose sense of itself as a community was as well defined as the Etonian old boy network. The distance from the officer's club in Burma to being invited as a "mate" to have a mug of cheap beer was one that Blair hoped to cross. He welcomed the recognition of himself as one of the poor, but rarely responded to it conversationally. His words would give him away. An Etonian's accent was not so easily shed as his clothes.

As the spring of 1928 neared, Blair planned his final move from artistic poverty to squalid poverty. He decided to move to Paris. He could live cheaply there, he spoke French, and there was, if he was interested, a large community of writers and artists residing in Paris. Blair thought that with what savings remained he could get a good amount of writing done, perhaps enough to break through into print. At the same time he could clarify his thoughts about poverty while finding a way of dealing with it in literary terms, and still manage to feed himself on a regular basis.

Upon arriving in Paris Blair stayed for a short while with his Aunt Nellie, one of Ida Limouzin's sisters. She called herself Nellie Adam, using the last name of the man with whom she lived, although they were not married. Nellie Adam had a fond spot for her nephew Eric, and Eugene Adam, her lover, liked the young man as well. Eugene and Nellie were, in their own way, bohemians themselves. It was clear that he would be welcome to stay with them, though the apartment was not spacious. Blair appreciated their kindness and the confidence they seemed to have in his literary ambitions; they, alone among his relatives, found nothing strange in a talented young man wanting to become a writer. He moved shortly to a room of his own, however, determined that he would make his way independently. Blair found an affordable and marginally comfortable spot in a tenement building at 6 Rue du Pot de Fer, a street lined with nearly identical buildings.

His new room was little different from the one he'd left in

London, and Blair was really no more or less poor at first than he'd been before. He was poor enough, though, surrounded by emigrés who had fled the Russian Revolution, by tradespeople, by students struggling for their education, by more than a few artists, and by many elderly people without funds. Rue du Pot de Fer was no artists' quarter, fashionably bohemian, but a shabby street on which poor people lived. They lived close to the bone, eking out a living as best they could, counting every coin and all too frequently finding themselves short.

Blair launched himself into his work. It was as though he were laying seige to editors in their castles. He not only wrote daily, but some days he did little else. Blair had not come to Paris to sit in sidewalk cafés and become lost in empty artistic conversation. He was in Paris to work, and he stuck to his purpose. He sat and smoked and typed, producing thousands of words a day. Blair began a novel about a drunken officer in Burma and the pages piled up quickly. He wrote quite a few short stories that he thought of as commercial, hoping to breach editorial resistance with at least one of them. He thought they were coming closer to the mark. At least his prose was growing cleaner, his style perhaps benefiting from Samuel Butler's warnings about literary adornment.

As his skills as a writer improved, so did Blair's approach to the marketing of his work. He was in no position to be snobbish, and avenues to print that he had previously avoided began to seem attractive. He read the lower-paying magazines even as he tried to sell to more lucrative markets. But the journalistic, political, and literary magazines, he noticed, appeared more frequently and were less opulently produced and easier to approach. He came across more than one piece that he was sure he could have done better. Fiction took time, even at his rapid pace, but journalistic pieces could be written quickly, speed offsetting low rates. Blair began to write nonfiction, literary and political journalism, articles, and essays. They came swiftly, if not easily. To increase his chances of publication—not to mention his chances of earning even a small amount—Blair submitted both to English and French publications. He worked on pieces about France, which he sent to Britain, and observations of British life, politics, and culture which he submitted to French periodicals. All of his work continued to come back.

It struck Blair that he might need professional assistance in placing his short stories, and he sent a package of the stories to an important London literary agent. This package, too, came back, but with a note full of good advice. The agent recommended that Blair try to relax a bit more while at the typewriter: there seemed to the agent to be too much *writer* and not enough story. Some of Blair's stories were too overtly sexual, or contained language too strong for the intended market. The stories showed promise, and if Blair would overcome his stylistic pretensions, the agent implied, he might be able to produce salable works.

Relaxation on the page, though, required even more alertness and concentration than did pretension. Purple prose and flowery phrases crept in too easily. Blair worked at simplifying his sentences, finding his way toward putting reality on the page, not just his version of good writing.

It was not simply descriptions of life among the poor that drew him, but the political roots of poverty as well. Blair did not restrict himself to poverty as a political theme. Politics shot through all of life, from the poor to the military to industry and even to the magazines he was trying to crack. There were political essays and article ideas everywhere, and as the political and economic ferment of the late twenties grew more intense, political magazines and newspapers were abundant. In September 1928, one of these, *Le Monde,* published in Paris, accepted a piece signed by E. A. Blair.

It was a brief article about the ways in which literary censorship was practiced in Britain. "La Censure en Angleterre," as the title read in French, appeared in the October 6, 1928 issue of *Le Monde,* seeming workmanlike and not out of place among the other columns of political and literary insight and rhetoric. Blair's article was easily read, his points about British prudery well presented, his conclusions about censorship both sensible and sound. "La Censure en Angleterre" was nothing spectacular. It was not the sort of debut to distract readers from more prestigious authors and more in-depth articles in the same issue. Its author even had to share a by-line with his translator. But the piece was publishable and it was published.

As 1929 neared, Blair had several sales to his credit. His short stories continued to be returned, but by New Year he was finding occasional markets for his articles in France and also in Britain. He was beginning to bolster his opinions with advocacy, offering courses of action as well as pointing out problems. Blair wrote of Burma, of literature, of the publishing industry, weaving political comment into his observations. He had not found yet the proper way of writing about the poor, but he continued to work on pieces about life in the depths as he had seen it. He sent copies of two novels to the agent in London, and labored at a long piece about his experiences among the poor; that piece looked more and more as if it would become a book. Blair's funds continued to diminish, and the journalism barely counted as income. A half-year after his first publication, he'd still earned less than £20 from full-time writing. Even poor Rue du Pot de Fer began to seem expensive to Blair. Occasionally he found employment as an English tutor, but that was irregular work and it paid little more than his articles.

By February 1929, the months of nonstop work combined with exposure to cold and poor nutrition to break Blair's health. He collapsed with pneumonia and was taken to Hôpital Cochin, a hospital for the poor. Hôpital Cochin was a teaching as well as a charity hospital, and many of the doctors were barely more than youths. They watched as the stream of patients waited endlessly to endure meaningless questions, a tepid sponging, a cursory examination, and assignment of a bed in a ward. Blair was given a nightshirt and thin robe, but the hospital had no sandals large enough for his feet, and he walked barefoot through the bitter February night in search of his ward and his bed.

When he found the ward it seemed more a place of condemnation than of hope. The beds were crowded side by side and virtually end to end, close enough for your neighbor's coughs to splash you. The screams of the cancer patient mingled with the coughs of the tubercular and the wailing of the amputee. The odors of disease, infection, and excrement overpowered any trace of medicinal odors, ultimately overwhelming the sense of smell itself. Working their way from bed to bed were a doctor and a student, drawing blood by creating a vacuum inside a small glass, then applying the heated glass to the patient in order to raise a blister. It was a medieval, agonizing practice, made worse when Blair witnessed the same glasses applied to him as had been used on the patient in the next bed. There was not even an attempt at sterilization, and the doctor and student seemed uninterested in anything Blair had to say. They seemed almost bored.

Cupping, as the procedure was called, had barely ended when Blair was seized by two nurses, who jerked him to a sitting position and applied a painful, burning poultice to his chest, strapping it behind his back so he could not remove it. Orderlies and attendants came to his bedside, an audience for his humiliation, their grinning faces and filthy clothes all Blair could see as the poultice was strapped in place. When the poultice was removed and Blair left to suffer alongside other sufferers, he had been in the hospital less than an hour.

He would stay for several weeks. Through his fever and pain he never forgot that he was a writer and never lost his powers of observation. He noticed everything. The scorn on the faces of the nurses as they told the patients to bathe themselves or remain dirty; the kindness of patients who bathed those not well enough to clean themselves. The decline of the minds of the dying until they lost control near the very end; the looks on their faces when they were dead; the hours the corpses lay in the ward until they were removed.

When Blair returned to Rue du Pot de Fer he was still weak, but he forced himself to write. He was not yet satisfied with his attempts at writing about oppression in Burma, but he knew now, more clearly than ever before, that there was oppression to be found outside his Paris room, and outside the similar room in London. Deathly ill, in stained robes identical to those still worn in death by nearby corpses, he'd *been* poor. Eric Blair, morally outraged, profoundly changed, and politically astute, realized that he had found in the lives and deaths of the poor not only a great theme, but also an important one.

Blair renewed his long stints at the typewriter, careful not to push too hard, building strength on the page while he marshaled his own physical strength. The markets were no more receptive to his work than they'd ever been. By summer his novels had been rejected and his short stories returned. He continued to circle around the narrative based on his experiences among the poor in Paris and as a tramp in London, seeking to find a proper form for it. Should it be a novel, an autobiography, or a journal? Blair searched through sentence after sentence for the right voice for this piece. He kept track of the pages as they piled up, and he measured his money against the calendar. As summer passed the calendar looked more and more ominous, a constant reminder of his state. He made it a practice to pay his rent a month in advance, enabling him to relax a bit. At least he had a place to stay for another month. But in late summer, with enough savings to see him through a few more weeks of writing, Blair's room was robbed and his money stolen. He had neither the time nor the energy to bemoan his loss: he was too busy just trying to survive. All that remained was what he had in his pockets.

Blair brushed his clothes, made himself look presentable, and went out in search of work. He found nothing, got through each day on pennies, but even his pennies ran out. He found himself joining a line of other poor Parisians and emigrés offering their clothes to pawnbrokers for a few francs. That was temporary relief at best, and without his good clothes, Blair stood no chance at all of finding a good job. He became a *plongeur,* a dishwasher in a cheap restaurant, earning a small wage, fighting for scraps of food left on diners' plates. He refused to see his aunt, lest she discover his situation and offer to help. He did not describe his circumstances in his infrequent letters home. He was poor.

Blair was also as observant as ever, perhaps more observant having passed through the period in the hospital. He'd seen how the poor lived, how they managed to exist through year after year of degradation, getting through each scrape somehow, until they, too, were staring corpses in a filthy hospital. He found allies: other artists, or would-be artists, exiled aristocrats who had a love of culture, communists who spurned society and spoke passionately of the revolution they planned, and how it would change the world. Blair listened intently, learning much. He discovered the radical zeal of the communists, but he also learned ways to smuggle luggage from a house where you could not pay the rent. He heard about the society of equals that was coming, and he was shown how to make a thin soup from a single potato. Some of his neighbors incited him to be more violent in his hatred of governments, to become more ardent in his condemnation of the world's powers. Other neighbors helped him blacken his ankles so that the holes in his socks would not be noticed when he interviewed for a job as a dishwasher. Blair took it all in.

As summer faded, he made ready to return to Britain. Blair contained his pride and borrowed his homeward fare from his Aunt Nellie. He'd been through nearly three months as a kitchen worker, and he remained willing to make sacrifices for his craft, but he knew too well the dangers of the Paris winter. By Christmas 1929, he was in Southwold with his family.

Richard Blair was nearly seventy-five by now, and Ida in her fifties. Blair was twenty-six, home again with his parents, and he could not escape seeing the disappointment, or at least confusion, in their eyes. What had he done? What could he point to as an accomplishment? His resignation from a respectable job in the police remained a thorn in the side of Richard

Blair. Hadn't he moved to Southwold because of its large population of retired people such as himself, who had spent all their working lives in India and other parts of the British Empire? A few articles in French newspapers and magazines, even fewer in English publications? Blair might show them with pride, but he still had earned less than £20 after nearly a year and a half as a full-time writer. His deep and genuine understanding of the poor made no impression on Richard and Ida Blair. They never made their disappointment blatant, and they offered no serious protest when Blair would don his ragged clothes and set out unexpectedly for a few days or weeks on the road as a tramp, living as an indigent. They listened to his boasts about the books he would write, but they saw no books.

The book, which Blair was calling *A Scullion's Diary*, occupied him throughout the spring of 1930. He was having trouble with its presentation, rewriting passages again and again, trying the work as fiction, as diary, as straight autobiography or reportage, as a mixture of more than one form. He accepted a job as a tutor, and when summer arrived, hired out as a tutor and traveling companion on more than one vacation. He carried the book with him as he taught and looked after his charges, and made clear to their parents that he thought of himself as a writer, and more than that, a writer about the poor. He did not want any misconceptions. Both his young students and their parents found him charming and gentle, and wished him well with his work.

The work included an increasing number of book reviews. Reviews paid even less than essays and journalism, but he had no trouble placing them. Editors began sending books to him, a steady stream of review requests that carried him through a biography of Herman Melville, a critical life of Alexander Pope, even a novel by J. B. Priestley, who wrote precisely the sort of commercial fiction that Blair had for so long tried to write. His reviews were clear, readable, offered a good understanding of the books under consideration, and presented Blair's opinions forcefully. Editors, pleased with the reviews, became more receptive to his articles. Blair began casting his tramping experiences in brief essays.

"The Spike" was one such essay, Blair's account of a weekend spent among other tramps in a "spike," a place where those with no money at all were given food and lodgings of a sort. Spikes possessed all the amenities of a prison, and they were run somewhat like prisons, with a major in charge, a search for contraband—cither money, tobacco, or alcohol—and visitors sleeping behind bars. Blair wrote the piece as a reminiscence by an anonymous narrator, an observer as well as a participant. The first-person voice helped Blair achieve his narrative goals: the story was related, the details were clear and striking, but the storyteller was largely absent. The reader knows little more about the narrator at the end of the piece than is known at the beginning. It was an approach that served Blair well.

"As always happens in the spike, I had at last managed to fall comfortably asleep when it was time to get up. The Tramp Major came marching down the passage with his heavy tread, unlocking the doors and yelling to us to show a leg. Promptly the passage was full of squalid shirt-clad figures rushing for the bathroom, for there was only one tub full of water between us all in the morning, and it was first come first served. When I arrived twenty tramps had already washed their faces. I gave one glance at the black scum on top of the water, and decided to go dirty for the day."

"The Spike" was accepted by *New Adelphi,* a literary and critical magazine Blair had mocked as pretentious while in Paris and even Burma, but whose quality, he thought, was improving. The *Adelphi,* as it was called, also printed several of his reviews. "The Spike," though, was Blair's first major piece to win acceptance, and he was satisfied with it. He liked the anonymous narrator, and would use the approach again, although he included a scene in "The Spike" that somewhat modified his purposes. Near the piece's conclusion, the narrator is recognized as

91

a "gentleman," although the recognition occupies only a few lines. But his prose had relaxed, and now he worked still harder at perfecting his style and approach.

A Scullion's Diary, Blair's long account of dishwashing in Paris, was completed in its first form by fall 1930. He typed a clean copy, but the manuscript was less than 40,000 words, barely a hundred pages. It was returned as too short by the publisher to whom Blair submitted it, and Blair undertook a revision. He searched his memory for incidents that could be included in the text, and expanded them in his imagination. The lines between fiction and autobiography grew more blurred with each draft of each page. As Blair began to write sections based upon his experiences as a tramp in Britain, 1931 unfolded around him, but he concentrated only upon his work. There was no doubt in his mind that he had the makings of a book, however much he might on occasion doubt his own ability to write that book.

While most of his concentration was focused upon his revision of *A Scullion's Diary,* Blair also turned back to Burma for material. His book would show life among the poor and oppressed from the inside, as it really was. He also forced himself to try to recreate what it had been like to be one of the oppressors, whether knowingly or not. Blair recalled the heat of Burma, the fury of the monsoons, the looks on the people's faces, his various postings. In Paris he had witnessed a man's death as a result of disease. In Burma, in uniform, Blair had witnessed more than one hanging. He distilled those experiences and applied himself and his new narrative approach to capturing a Burmese execution on paper.

His pared-down style proved as effective against a Burmese backdrop as a British or a French one. On the page he created time and he created place. Blair called up conversations overheard, or that he had imagined he overheard. He made a picture for himself, and for his readers, of the prisoner and the executioners. And as the piece, which he called "A Hanging," took shape, Eric Blair began to play detail against detail, keeping the reader aware that a man's life is about to be ended at imperial whim, but showing the reader more trivial and poignant detail as well.

"It was about forty yards to the gallows. I watched the bare brown back of the prisoner marching in front of me. He walked clumsily with his bound arms, but quite steadily, with that bobbing gait of the Indian who never straightens his knees. At each step his muscles slid neatly into place, the lock of hair on his scalp danced up and down, his feet printed themselves on the wet gravel. And once, in spite of the men who gripped him by each shoulder, he stepped lightly aside to avoid a puddle on the path.

"It is curious, but till that moment I had never realised what it means to destroy a healthy, conscious man."

"A Hanging" appeared in the August 1931 issue of the *Adelphi*, signed Eric A. Blair. Its author was in Kent picking hops. He was earning only a few coins a week, and by the middle of September he had returned to London. This time he did not wait for memory to alter his perceptions, and perhaps deepen them. He immediately began a long journal called "Hop-Picking." His typewriter rattled through the end of September and on into October, as he produced dozens of pages of detail and description. The piece did not find a market.

As a means of making money he offered his services to publishers as a translator, even suggesting French novels that he thought worthy of English editions. Blair received no assignments as translator, although he had a brief correspondence with the poet T. S. Eliot, who was one of the directors of Faber and Faber, one of the most prestigious British publishers.

Blair himself was working at very little other than his writing. He took on occasional jobs as a laborer, working in fish markets, but nothing more substantial. Earnings from his typewriter remained miniscule. From time to time his parents, despite their disapproval of Blair's actions, gave him a pound or two, and he went to other relatives for long visits. His brother-in-law, Marjorie's husband, had taught Blair to fish when the two were growing up, but now he saw Blair as a vagrant, an idler, a man too lazy or unambitious to accept his normal responsibilities.

As Christmas 1931 approached, Blair, in a mood of resentment and self-pity, decided to pass the Christmas holiday behind bars. He set about getting himself arrested as a drunk, got drunk and was picked up, but was released all too soon the same afternoon. He had no better luck in other locations, either as a drunk or as a beggar, both of which postures were illegal. He could not get himself arrested.

The new year began and Blair at last decided to seek employment. There seemed at the time little more he could learn about the poor, or observe among them, and his life of subsistence required more energy than would an undemanding job. His narrative account of life among poor Parisians and of London from the viewpoint of an articulate tramp was making the rounds of publishers. Blair called the book *Days in London and Paris,* but expanded, better written, more incisive and readable, it had no better luck than as *A Scullion's Diary.* T. S. Eliot rejected the book for Faber and Faber late in February 1932. Less than two months later, Eric Blair was a teacher at The Hawthorns, a school for boys.

The Hawthorns was no St. Cyprian's. For all of that school's faults, its students were young people of promise. The Hawthorns prepared its graduates for lives as clerks. The material to be covered was dreary and repetitive, but Blair settled into the job with some enthusiasm. He hated the idea of having to work rather than write, but he enjoyed working with children and was generous with the time he spent with his students.

Time not engaged by the students was passed in his room, typing. It was different to be in a dry and almost warm room, with a full stomach from a meal taken in a dining room with colleagues: a far step from his life in the streets. But Blair was aware that The Hawthorns was a stopping place at which he could catch his breath, regain his strength and financial reserves, even get some writing done. He was not tempted to relax his literary ambitions. Too many schools like The Hawthorns held too many teachers who had intended to become writers or poets or composers. It was a banal and empty sort of existence, its result being teaching of even lower quality than he recalled from St. Cyprian's. Blair also found himself using his cane more than once, striking a student as Mr. Wilkes had struck him. As though in contrition, he became more enthusiastic than other teachers, devising contests and awarding prizes to students who excelled.

As Blair struggled to come to terms with his first steady employment in years, his agent continued to show *Days in London and Paris* to publishers, discussing its excellence with editors. While Blair taught, wrote reviews, fished, and gardened, *Days in London and Paris* made its way to Victor Gollancz, an important and aggressive publisher with a reputation for iconoclasm as well as an enthusiasm for books that served left-wing political causes. In April the book was recommended by one of Gollancz's readers, and in June 1932 Blair was notified that Victor Gollancz was eager to publish the book.

There was a good amount of editorial work to be done. Blair wrote honestly, but many of the scenes and much of the conversation and dialogue in *Days in London and Paris* proved too strong for publication in 1932. Gollancz and Blair met soon after the book was accepted, and discussed the necessary editing in detail. Gollancz also requested a new, more dramatic title for the book. Blair considered calling it *The Lady Poverty*, or *Lady Poverty*. He was also searching for a new by-line. The book, it was agreed, would be published as a novel.

Less than a month after Gollancz agreed to publish *Days in London and Paris*, Blair wrote to his agent that he wished the book to be published under a pseudonym. He felt himself to be in a good position to make such a request: any name would sell books as well as the unknown Eric Blair. He continued to write literary and journalistic pieces over his own name, but he would not sign that name to his book. It contained many episodes, even edited, that would shock readers of its time, and Blair had no wish to embarrass his parents. He was not certain whether a pen name would be permanent, or used only on this one book.

With a journalistic reminiscence done, Blair was hard at work on a full-fledged novel. He set the book in Burma, and though the interest expressed by publishers pleased him, he could not promise when it would be completed. He continued to teach, and he wrote in the evenings, producing essays, book reviews, and articles, saving hard work on the novel for holidays when he could get at it for uninterrupted stretches.

This way of life continued throughout the fall of 1932. Blair dealt with the myriad details that accompany publication: editing, but also checking for libel, clarifying points, and proofreading. He suggested *The Confessions of a Dishwasher* as a title, but remained unsatisfied. The whole book dissatisfied him, he made clear to friends. He thought of it as an apprentice piece written so long ago that he barely recalled it. He was more interested in his novel, and while he would be pleased to have the book out, he was just as pleased to have kept his own name clear from it. Among the names to which he gave consideration were the ordinary Kenneth Miles and the unusual H. Lewis Allways. He preferred a more ordinary name, a simple and strong name, but one that attracted no attention to himself.

Eric Blair had spent the previous Christmas seeking to be arrested. As Christmas 1932 arrived, he received the first copies of his first book. The title finally settled upon seemed strong and accurate. The book was called *Down and Out in Paris and London.* The by-line it carried was a name as plain and simple as his own, a good name for a writer. The book was signed by George Orwell.

SIX

ORWELL

HE REMAINED, AND THOUGHT of himself as, Eric Blair, but he learned that a pseudonym can quickly create a life of its own. When reviews began to arrive, and he chose to acknowledge or respond to them, how should he sign his letters? Signing Eric Blair would give away the whole game, not to mention jeopardizing his job should the book prove controversial. But to sign George Orwell raised problems of its own. Was he accepting an alter ego, even if only a literary one? The pen name was no closely held secret—pieces of *Down and Out* had been derived from published articles that had been signed by Eric Blair, and literary detectives would not face too much of a mystery in putting the two together. But who was to become the important writer? Whose name, finally, would appear on the "collected edition" that the young author so rarely thought of any more? Closer to the present, should Blair's or Orwell's name go on the novel of Burma that was in the typewriter?

Down and Out in Paris and London settled those questions. It was no world-shaking success, but at least initially the book did well. Before *Down and Out* had been in the stores a month its 1,500 copy first printing was gone, and a second printing of 500 copies had been ordered. As the second month passed another 1,000 copies were printed. In America, Harper Brothers printed 1,750 copies, but no second printing was required. While its surge did not last in Britain, the book did sell well for an author's first book, and it became clear to Orwell that his pen name would be used on his novel. Gollancz pointed out that though *Down and Out* was no bestseller, it had introduced George Orwell to the book reviewers and to a few thousand book buyers. Eric Blair remained unknown, except by his friends. Socially, he used his own name throughout his life.

Orwell was pleased with the book's sales, and even more pleased with the reviews, which were generally favorable. He saw his name and his book mentioned in newspapers and magazines where he had reviewed other writers' works. J. B. Priestley commended *Down and Out in Paris and London.* More than one critic praised the style of the book, noting the effectiveness of its quiet, straightforward narrative manner. Readers and reviewers seemed to realize from the first few pages that they were in the presence of a real talent, a writer who not only wrote clearly, but also had seen corners of the world they could only imagine.

Mingled with the praise were occasional criticisms that expressed doubt about Orwell's own poverty. Wasn't he just an affluent person traveling among the poor in disguise, some critics asked. Orwell made no response to such reviews, but when the veracity of his account of restaurant kitchens was questioned, he wrote a letter to *The Times* maintaining that every filthy practice he mentioned was true, and had been witnessed during his days as a dishwasher. The letter, which appeared late in January 1933, was signed George Orwell, with the pseudonym coyly enclosed in quotation marks.

Orwell's family in Southwold was not surprised that he had made a book out of his experiences, but their reaction to its contents and especially its frank language made Orwell certain the pen name had been a sound decision. He had no wish to embarrass anyone. He knew as well that his Burmese novel would be equally frank, drawing an unflattering portrait of the workings of empire. His parents seemed more baffled than hurt, but Blair wished to cause no pain at all.

He continued to put in long hours at the novel, but would give his agent no projection of when it would be finished. Orwell was eager to pursue writing full time once more, but *Down and Out in Paris and London* would earn him barely more than one hundred pounds. While that was rare wealth when compared to his days in Paris, he was not yet prepared to abandon teaching. Little would be accomplished by surrendering the security of the job at The Hawthorns and returning to a cheap room while his savings were eaten away. Orwell's agent, Leonard Moore, had shown some enthusiasm for the first hundred pages of the Burmese novel, and Orwell resolved to hold on to his teaching position until that novel was completed and published. Perhaps then he would be able to devote all of his time to writing while still living in some comfort at least.

Gradually the initial feeling of exuberance Orwell had experienced at the publication of *Down and Out in Paris and London* faded. Teaching became more and more drudgery, and the evenings and weekends of work on the novel became bouts with frustration. For all of his struggles with *Down and Out,* and his uncertainties about form and style through that book's many drafts, Orwell found his new manuscript to be far more difficult. Although *Down and Out* was categorized by publishers and critics as a novel, and many of the incidents it contained were fictionalized, the book was less a work of fiction than Orwell's amalgamation of fiction, nonfiction, and reminiscence. Its accomplishment was measured against his own memories and observations; he had in his past experience a good gauge of the book's effectiveness.

With his Burmese novel, however, Orwell measured his success not only against his memories of Burma, but also against the success of novels he admired. Orwell was attempting to write a literary novel, lush with language, a story created in his imagination, tempered by his control of technique. He'd read novels all his life, had studied them and reviewed them, and understood the requirements and demands made of an effective piece of fiction. But most days his achievement at the typewriter fell far short of his intention and desire, and few of the passages satisfied him. There were whole sections of the book he felt were unworthy of comparison even with cheap potboilers. He found himself becoming bogged down in too much language, not enough story, or too much story without sufficient characterization. He wrote and rewrote. Having become a demanding critic of other writer's works, Orwell held himself to the same high standards, lapsing into depression when he failed to meet them.

The ferment and revolution of the nineteen twenties and early thirties extended to literature as well as politics, and even as he sought to master the art of the conventional, naturalistic novel, Orwell was aware of the changes that had overtaken literature. Writers such as Virginia Woolf and James Joyce had probed farther into human psychology than more traditional novelists, with Joyce stretching the limits of language and narrative in an attempt to present the thoughts of ordinary people on the page in an extraordinary way. Ernest Hemingway, himself an expatriate American who had lived poorly in Paris not long before Orwell, had stripped language to a spare and cadenced simplicity, and by that approach sought to put reality in print. Other Americans, John Dos Passos and William Faulkner, were using stream of consciousness techniques—attempts to recreate thought in written language—or cinematic techniques to further extend the range of novelistic effects. D. H. Lawrence, more traditional in form than other contemporary novelists, had pushed farther into the nature of sexuality than others, and was trying to break down barriers against language considered obscene. Aldous Huxley, whom Orwell recalled as a French instructor at Eton, had built a reputation during the twenties for sharp, satirical novels resonant with the emptiness that afflicted many following World War I. The art of novel writing was changing.

George Orwell, though, pursued a more traditional path as he shaped his first novel. He knew his strengths and weaknesses, and endeavored to build a novel around the strengths. Orwell had great admiration for *Ulysses,* James Joyce's masterpiece, and recommended it to friends while it was still illegal to own a copy of *Ulysses* in Britain. But for all his acute understanding of Joyce's accomplishment, Orwell felt himself more technically limited. He wanted his novel to possess realistic, memorable characters, to move through a plot that provided readers with a sense of pattern and structure, and to be well written. Coupled with these three challenges—that sound far easier to meet than they are in reality—was the dilemma of coming to terms with Burma. Orwell did not want to lose his story or his characters in a mass of symbolism, but he did wish to create a novel that synthesized his feelings about imperialism, as well as his own experience of it.

Orwell set the book in northern Burma, away from the Irrawaddy Delta where he had passed so much disagreeable time. He was not interested in writing a novel solely about the Imperial Police, and created a protagonist, James Flory, who was a timber merchant. Orwell wrote in the third person, putting distance between himself and his central character.

Not that *Burmese Days,* as Orwell called the novel, was an objective portrait of the empire in Burma. Despite his agonies during the book's composition, Orwell's long-simmering anger, resentment, and hatred gave him a power on the page that was clear from the opening chapter. *Burmese Days* was intended as a novel, and it certainly succeeded as one, but Orwell's opinions, political and moral, shaped every passage. Even character descriptions and introductions carried political weight. U Po Kyin, the corrupt and manipulative Burmese civil servant with whom the novel opens, is presented matter-of-factly as a man who understands the best way of coexisting with the empire; it was an understanding he had possessed since childhood, when "In his childish way he had grasped that his own people were no match for this race of giants. To fight on the side of the British, to become a parasite upon them, had been his ruling ambition, even as a child."

Flory, around whom *Burmese Days* revolved, was also introduced by way of his relationship to the empire and its power and customs. The reader is made aware of Flory's problem with alcohol, but almost immediately Orwell enlarged the reader's perspective. Flory's home was near the real seat of empire. "Beyond that was the European Club, and when one looked at the Club—a dumpy one-storey wooden building—one looked at the real centre of the town. In any town in India the European Club is the spiritual citadel, the real seat of the British power, the Nirvana for which native officials and millionaires pine in vain. It was doubly so in this case, for it was the proud boast of the Kyauktada Club that, almost alone of Clubs in Burma, it had never admitted an Oriental to membership."

That segregation, and the setting of Kyauktada as one of the final Burmese communities to abandon old imperial customs in view of the rising tide of Burmese nationalism and anti-imperialism, gave Orwell the dramatic tension for his novel. He kept his prose low-key, almost laconic in places, occasionally lapsing into floridity as though recreating with words the thick overgrowth of the jungle. But even the purple passages of *Burmese Days* read well, and as spring 1933 gave way to summer, Orwell began to fill with excitement at the thought of finishing the book. He sent sections of the manuscript to friends, along with apologetic covering letters in which he explained that the book needed a rewrite, that it was nowhere near so good as it would be after a summer spent strengthening it.

He was writing love letters as well, having become enamored of Eleanor Jaques, a friend from Southwold with whom he'd often discussed literature. Orwell's interest in her deepened, and he composed long letters to Eleanor, courting her in the same fashion as he had Jacintha Buddicom when he was younger. He thanked Eleanor for every kindness, wrote of how he missed her, asked if they might meet on occasions to walk together or make love. Orwell had no more success with this romance by mail than he had with the previous one, and Eleanor married someone else the next year. Although Orwell enjoyed occasional dalliances and even short affairs with women, he entered his early thirties with no serious romantic prospects.

It appeared briefly that spring that his financial prospects would be equally bleak. The Hawthorns had run upon the harsh facts of the Depression, the school was being sold, and Orwell was out of a job. He may have looked upon the school's collapse as a blessing, for to become a full-time writer as a result of an employer's default was far different from casting off a steady job in order to write. Orwell's unemployment was short lived, however, and he was hired to teach at Frays College in Uxbridge in southeastern England. Frays was considerably larger than The Hawthorns, with an enrollment that approached two hundred students, both boys and girls. Orwell's position—he was hired as Eric Blair, of course—was to begin in September, giving him the summer to work on *Burmese Days.*

He did not complete the novel during his vacation, and took the manuscript with him to Uxbridge. Orwell spent his days teaching, but in the evening, when the other instructors gathered around a fire to talk and unwind, Orwell went quickly to his room where he'd set up his typewriter. The pages came no more easily than ever, but they came steadily, as Orwell built his vision of the British Empire, and its decline as a result of its own nature. No one in the novel escaped his caustic, critical eye. The Burmese were as corrupt as the British, the merchants as bad as the military. It was not a question of the British Empire being bad; it was, Orwell made clear, an unavoidable fact of imperialism that all whom it touched were corrupted. Throughout the fall of 1933 he put his characters through their paces, moving the plot toward its tragic, inescapable end.

Occasionally he took an afternoon or a weekend off for relaxation. His fellow teachers recalled knocks at their doors and the sight of Orwell with a string of fresh fish presented as a gift. Some evenings, perhaps weary of the novel or simply out of a sense of decorum, he joined the others in their common room. He did a bit of gardening. At the dinner table Orwell proved a pleasant, wide-ranging conversationalist, annoying his companions, though, by smoking cigarettes while others ate. Orwell was only rarely without a cigarette, despite a chronic cough, and had mastered the talent of rolling his own cigarettes one-handed, leaving his other hand free to gesture as he spoke.

That fall Orwell took some of his savings and bought another motorcycle. He took advantage of his increased mobility to travel throughout the area, often with his fishing rod strapped to the motorcycle. The days grew colder and Orwell continued to go on occasional rides, buttoning his jacket around him but wearing no overcoat. He finished *Burmese Days* early in December and not long afterward was on a motorcycle jaunt when he was soaked to the skin by a winter rain. He caught pneumonia, and once more his health collapsed.

The hospital in Uxbridge was clean and crisp, run with British efficiency. But during the delirium that accompanied his high fever, Orwell called out to his nurses again and again that he was worried about his money. As a tramp he'd learned to sleep with his funds clutched beneath his pillow; sick and hospitalized he knew only that the space beneath his pillow was empty. His nightmare fears passed along with his fever, and despite the deathwatch to which Ida and Avril Blair had been summoned, Orwell began to regain his health. His physicians made it clear that he was not strong enough to resume his teaching duties, and Blair, his novel done and its sale, he was certain, imminent, took the opportunity to become a full-time writer. Shortly after New Year 1934, Orwell returned to Southwold to live with his parents as he completed his recuperation and began his career in earnest.

As January passed, Orwell's health improved, but his spirits were dampened by the response to *Burmese Days*. Victor Gollancz rejected the book, informing Orwell's agent that he was too frightened of possible libel suits to publish it in good conscience. Heinemann, another important publisher of novels, rejected *Burmese Days* for similar reasons. The novel was fiction, but Orwell had drawn upon his memories, and written clearly and bitingly. His novel's portrait of colonial life was so scathing that it seemed likely to provoke lawsuits from readers who saw or thought they saw themselves unfavorably portrayed in its pages.

Burmese Days was too strong for English publishers to accept, but Harpers agreed to publish an American edition if Orwell would make some changes in the manuscript. The revisions were intended to reduce the possibility of lawsuits, and Blair made them quickly. *Burmese Days* was scheduled for American publication in the fall of 1934. British publishers remained uninterested.

In Southwold, Orwell had begun a new novel, this one set in England, with a female protagonist. He wanted to produce a work of fiction more fully imaginative than *Burmese Days*. Orwell also gave himself the task of writing a more experimental novel, in which a variety of literary techniques and strategies could be employed to unfold the story and investigate its heroine's psychology. Dorothy Hare, Orwell's character, was the spinsterish daughter of an Anglican clergyman, a woman whose life was composed of little defeats and no victories: her existence is ruled by her father's demands, the demands of her faith, the propriety of the small English village in which she lives. Orwell wrote the first hundred pages or so of the novel rapidly and easily. He was confident in his creation of Dorothy and in his imagination of her surroundings.

Having set the novelistic stage, though, he dramatically altered it by having Dorothy stricken with amnesia as a result of a pass made at her by an unwanted suitor. Dorothy Hare wanted no suitors, and although Orwell did not become explicit in the novel, the kiss on the cheek that Dorothy received was an almost arbitrary gimmick, used to propel her from her safe existence into a life on the road, down and out as Orwell himself had been, a middle-class woman living among the poor and the rough. Orwell returned to his own experiences as sources for scenes, putting Dorothy to work as a hop picker and having her experience life in the slums. Even as he created the scenes, Orwell made it clear to his friends that he thought the book was in trouble. Its plot seemed too arbitrary, Dorothy's motivations so nebulous as to be invisible. He could not abandon the book, though; he was desperate to have a novel published in Britain. The summer of 1934 passed as Orwell pressed on.

By October the book was complete, Dorothy's amnesia cured, and the restored Dorothy returned to her father. Orwell called the book *A Clergyman's Daughter*, and he was not proud of it. Some of the passages seemed almost slavishly imitative of techniques introduced by James Joyce. Other sections made little sense. The entire plot still struck Orwell as a good idea, and amnesia an interesting fulcrum on which to turn a plot, but he wrote his agent of his dissatisfaction with the novel. He did not offer to revise the book, and instead planned other projects. A poem, "On a Ruined Farm near the His Master's Voice Gramophone Factory," had appeared in the *Adelphi*, and was selected for inclusion in a book called *The Best Poems of 1934*. He wrote some reviews, and for a while gave thought to writing a brief biography of Mark Twain, although he could not find a publisher for the project. During October *Burmese Days* was published in America, with Harper Brothers using the fear of libel and its rejection by British publishers as an advertising ploy to attract readers seeking controversy or sensation. The ploy did not work well, for although the book was favorably reviewed, it sold few copies.

Orwell had stayed long enough in Southwold, but had no interest in resuming a teaching career. That fall he found a job as a clerk in a bookshop in London, perhaps thinking that proximity to so many works of literature would have a beneficial effect on his own work. The error in such thoughts became clear after only a short while as an employee of Booklovers' Corner. There were rows of shelves and tables crammed with thousands of books of all sorts. The books blended together in Orwell's vision until it was possible to lose sight of them as individual titles possessed of worth, and see them only as a great dusty mass, unwanted good books no better than unwanted bad ones. Orwell felt his affection for books as physical objects begin to fade.

Nor were bookbuyers or browsers any better. While Orwell met more than a few people who shared his love of literature and with whom he became friends, most of his meetings with them took place outside the bookshop. Many of those with whom he felt sympathy were writers like himself, struggling up, or artists or students. The customers Orwell encountered while working in Booklovers' Corner were not interested in literature, and for the most part they were not interested in reading. Some of them entered the shop to purchase a gift for a relative, and expected the clerk to know exactly the sort of book that would be appropriate. Others came in, paid their pennies of rental for a temporary loan of a book, and were never seen again, doubtless taking the volume and selling it to another bookstore in another part of London. There were customers who bought books by the yard, books that would furnish a room but would never be opened and read. The majority of customers were those who entered the store simply as a means of escaping the elements, browsing for hours until the weather cleared or the shop closed, never purchasing anything. Within the walls of the Booklovers' Corner Orwell began to feel like a prisoner choking on dust.

His growing distaste for books as artifacts did not interfere with Orwell's own literary ambitions. The one good thing about the bookshop job was that he worked only during the afternoons; the early hours and evening hours were devoted to his typewriter, which he set up in the room he lived in above the bookstore. He was already at work on another novel, again set in England, in a bookstore, with a protagonist who was a struggling writer, bitter about his fate.

Orwell was still struggling, but less bitter than many writers he met. Gollancz had accepted *A Clergyman's Daughter* in spite of its flaws and despite its author's reservations. The publishers did insist on a series of changes to make the book less likely to provoke lawsuits from people who imagined themselves caricatured in its pages. Orwell was by now accustomed to such editorial work, if not enthusiastic about it. There had been no lawsuits over the American edition of *Burmese Days*, and with

107

that seeming a good omen, Gollancz asked to see the book again. Orwell sent him a copy and Gollancz at last agreed to publish a British edition, but only after further editorial surgery and careful examination by attorneys.

A Clergyman's Daughter appeared in March 1934, in an edition of 4,000 copies that sold moderately well, although no second printing was required. Orwell announced to his friends that he was embarrassed by the book, that its amateurishness disgusted him, and that he had written the story of Dorothy Hare and her amnesia only as a means of making money. Now he wanted from the literary public a sort of amnesia of its own. He wished his second novel to be forgotten, and boasted that he would not allow it to be reprinted even if demand for the book grew. The demand did not grow, and more than a few reviewers took Orwell to task for the clumsiness with which he manipulated his heroine. Orwell tried to ignore the reviews and get on with newer, better work.

Orwell had moved that March from his room above the bookstore to a small flat not too far away. With his second novel just published in England, and his first due belatedly in June, Orwell felt a growing sense of well-being, of strengthened powers. His income had not yet risen, but it surely would. More importantly, he'd continued to write throughout the difficult years just past, and had continued, in spite of problems that would have discouraged many writers, to publish his writings. He began to overcome some of his shyness. He made friends with his landlady, Rosalind Obermeyer, who was studying for an advanced degree in psychology at London's University College. Together with Mrs. Obermeyer, Orwell decided to give a small party, and they each made up their guest lists. Orwell invited friends from the literary community, and his landlady invited some of her fellow students, including a young woman named Eileen O'Shaughnessy. Eileen was two years younger than Orwell, an honors English graduate who, after a wide variety of experiences in teaching and business, had returned to school with the goal of earning a master's degree in psychology. Dark haired and pretty, as well as opinionated, articulate, and intelligent, Eileen O'Shaughnessy captured Orwell's attention at the party, and he passed much of the evening in conversation with her. Within a few days he was accompanying Eileen on horseback rides and long walks, and he even mentioned to some of his friends that she was the sort of woman he could marry.

Marriage was on his creative mind as well as in his romantic thoughts. Orwell's new novel was taking shape, and his protagonist, Gordon Comstock, was a minor poet torn between clinging to his artistic gifts, and scorning the material world, or returning to copywriting in order to marry the woman he loved. Orwell set the novel up carefully, making Comstock just enough of a success—one small book of half-good poems, a long poem in the works—to make his artistic pretensions believable. But he made him just enough of a failure—Comstock spent more time moaning about his writing than he did writing—to make the middle-class temptation ultimately unavoidable. The novel moved along smooth tracks, scene after scene drawing the contrast between Comstock's goals and the middle-class world his fiancée desires. Comstock, working in a bookstore, trying to write, feeling his vision and strength to resist fading simultaneously, was a marvelous creation.

It was not, however, a portrait of George Orwell, and the bitter account of Comstock and Rosemary was no description of Orwell's courtship of Eileen O'Shaughnessy. By fall 1935, Orwell and Eileen were discussing marriage, but there was never any question of Orwell abandoning his literary career. For one thing, despite his low income, Orwell's career was off to a good start, and continued to give promise of a brighter future. For another, Eileen was as independent and committed to ideas as was the man she would marry. They came from similar backgrounds—both of their fathers had been civil servants. While neither was interested in joining wholeheartedly the pursuit of profit that characterized the middle-class world as Gordon Comstock saw it, neither were they eager to starve for art or an ideal. Orwell had starved, perhaps deliberately, for the sake of experience, and Eileen had seen enough thin days to be unwilling to marry Orwell until her education was complete and his income increased. Those prospects, though, seemed achievable. *Burmese Days* appeared in Britain and quickly sold out its 2,500-copy first printing, earning generally favorable reviews, one of them from Orwell's schoolmate Cyril Connolly, now becoming established as an influential critic. Connolly's name, in fact, was better known than Orwell's; the two had maintained only sporadic contact since Eton. Victor Gollancz, despite his fears of litigation, continued to believe in Orwell as a writer of promise. Orwell, hard at work on a novel about a would-be writer who lacked the determination to stick to it, continued to believe in himself.

As the pages of his new novel grew into a thick pile beside his typewriter that fall, Orwell began to cast about for a fitting title. Gordon Comstock lacked enough confidence to succeed as a poet, or enough anger to resist the invitation of the "money-god," as Orwell called it. He also lacked enough self-control to keep from impregnating Rosemary, and found himself increasingly drawn toward a predictable life in a small flat, with wife and children, a job as an advertising copywriter. This lack of individuality was perhaps compensated for by a sense of community with other, identical, households. All such households had their lace curtains, and their front windows all held huge aspidistra plants. Those plants became a symbol, and at the novel's cynical but conventionally happy ending, Gordon Comstock, his poetic vision abandoned, is seized by a final, social vision.

"Our civilisation is founded on greed and fear, but in the lives of common men the greed and fear are mysteriously transmuted into something nobler. The lower middle-class people in there, behind their lace curtains, with their children and their scraps of furniture and their aspidistras—they lived by the money-code, sure enough, and yet they contrived to keep their decency. The money-code as they interpreted it was not merely cynical and hoggish. They had their standards, their inviolable points of honour. They 'kept themselves respectable'—kept the aspidistra flying. Besides, they were *alive*. They were bound up in the bundle of life. They begot children, which is what the saints and the soul-savers never by any chance do.

"The aspidistra is the tree of life, he thought suddenly."

And so Gordon Comstock abandoned one dream, trading it for another that seemed to Comstock neither better nor worse, his artistic intent and commitment being far less serious than that of his creator. In this reverie, Orwell found the title of his novel; he called it *Keep the Aspidistra Flying*, and finished it late in 1935. He'd railed against the money-god, but as it related to his characters, not in any political way or as an angry indictment of a social system. The novel was no *Burmese Days*. Its focus was too tight for that. And even as Orwell wrote of Comstock's failure to overcome his attraction to the money-god, Orwell moved from the flat rented from Rosalind Obermeyer, a bit embarrassed to be so poor as to rent from one of Eileen's fellow students. When he and Eileen dined out, infrequently, Orwell insisted on paying the check himself, and often worried throughout the meal whether he had sufficient funds. He wore a loose-fitting sportcoat and baggy flannel trousers—Eileen wore suits that were the female equivalent—but both Orwell's and Eileen's clothes were of good quality. They were caught, in their own way, as was Comstock: critical of the middle class but ineradicably of it, captured in a contradiction of which they were aware, neither fasting nor feasting, but somewhere on the low end in between.

Victor Gollancz accepted *Keep the Aspidistra Flying* without hesitation and scheduled the book for publication in spring 1936. Early that year Orwell gave up his job in Booklovers' Corner and started looking for a new writing project. He continued to do reviews and articles, but with Eileen's graduation approaching he wanted to write another novel, something more ambitious and potentially more successful, as a means of breaking out of his economic trap. He could not marry Eileen until he had enough money, and the only way he saw of earning enough money was by writing. He gave some thought to a long novel, perhaps a story that spanned several generations.

Orwell's plans were interrupted by Victor Gollancz. In addition to being an important publisher, Gollancz was an important figure in Britain's political left. He gave time, money, and his personal prestige to a variety of left-wing causes, and in early 1936 he had become intrigued by the nature of unemployment in Britain. Mines, factories, and mills had closed as a result of the Depression, and unemployment was reaching disastrous levels. Gollancz wanted to publish a report on conditions in northern England, an industrial area. What was it like there now, Gollancz wanted to know. How did men and women who'd worked all their lives cope with the failure of their employers? What were their political feelings? Could socialism solve their problems, and Britain's problems, too? Gollancz sent for Orwell.

The topic seemed perfect for the author of *Down and Out in Paris and London* and the essays about life among the working poor and the tramps. Gollancz was willing to give Orwell free rein to do his own investigation, and to develop the proper format for the book that would follow. Orwell was certainly up to the challenge, enthusiastic about the project even before he learned Gollancz's terms. For his report on the conditions in the north of England, George Orwell would receive an advance of £500, the largest of his career, and a large advance for writers far more successful than Orwell. It was enough money to last Orwell and Eileen a year or two, and they could begin to plan their wedding.

But first Orwell had to make his investigation, and in late January he set out on the road once more, eager to learn, open to new experiences, not quite certain what he would find.

SEVEN

THE ROAD TO DISILLUSIONMENT

HE TRAVELED BY TRAIN at first, but soon traveled on foot or in crowded public buses, means of transportation that brought him closer to the unemployed. Orwell kept careful notes as he traveled north, taking in not only attitude and opinion, but being diligent about collecting facts with which to support his writing. He slept in lodging houses—barely a step up from the rooms he'd taken in Paris or the poor sections of London. Orwell seemed determined at first to find as much filth as he could. He would claim later that he tolerated the dirt and odor well enough, until he sat at the breakfast table one morning and discovered a full chamber pot under the table near his chair. He took to staying with the unemployed workers, in their own homes, which he found to be quite clean. It was a matter of pride to many of the unemployed that while there might be no income, there would be no squalor. By February 1936 Orwell was in Manchester, ready to begin his work.

Orwell had been provided with a number of contacts in the area, and had letters of introduction from mutual acquaintances in London. He called first upon the man who supervised the printing of the *Adelphi,* and who was an insightful and influential local labor leader. Through talking with him, Orwell could begin sorting out the various political and social factions seeking the support of the unemployed. There seemed to be dozens of such groups, some large, some small, all vocal. Their anger was directed at a government that had failed in its responsibilities to the unemployed, although the groups differed as to what those responsibilities were, and how they should be carried out. What they did agree upon was that the attempts made so far to deal with relief for the unemployed had either been ill-considered or incompetent. Change was demanded.

But whose change? Among the most influential of the political groups was the Independent Labour Party (ILP), which had been founded in 1893 and had developed close ties with labor unions. The ILP had broken with the politically established Labour Party in 1932. The ILP had never been so rarefied an intellectual body as the contemporaneous Fabian Society, which boasted among its membership at various times George Bernard Shaw, H. G. Wells, Beatrice and Sidney Webb, and other leading left-wing thinkers and writers. In fact, much of the ILP's intellectual core had refused to join in the split from the Labour Party and had formed another organization, the Socialist League. The ILP might lack a large intellectual core, but it attracted the attention of many working men and women, and it was not without an interest in ideas: theories of reform were as frequent a topic as unemployment statistics.

Also making its presence known in industrially depressed areas was the Communist Party, increasingly loud and exhortatory, but whose actual hold over the workers was difficult for Orwell to gauge. The National Unemployed Workers' Movement (NUWM) had been formed to give an additional voice to those out of work. (The unions whose members were joining NUWM objected to it, perhaps fearing it would weaken them.) Communist influence in the administration of NUWM was strong. Some right-wing commentators said that it was a communist organization. National Unemployed Workers' Movement members staged hunger marches on London in an attempt to demonstrate not only the plight of the unemployed, but also their comradeship.

As is customary during hard times, churches also became more active, some of them growing political, others remaining sure that faith alone would provide an answer. The more energetic churchmen campaigned as vigorously for members as did the political organizations.

Orwell soon discovered that many of the workers he met belonged to more than one organization. If there was an overlap among the groups, there was also great disagreement among them, with no two alike in their prescriptions for Britain's ills. It was not enough simply to be left wing. Questions arose: Left of what? How far left? More left than what? But disgust, anger, and disappointment were emotions that everyone agreed upon. Political speakers shouted that theirs was the voice of the majority, but their shouts were never echoed by a majority's cheers.

It was recommended to Orwell that he travel farther north, to Wigan in the coal-mining heart of Lancashire, close to Manchester. He made the trip to Wigan, aware that he could be perceived as merely another middle-class Londoner, wearing studiously baggy clothes, come to talk about his solidarity with the lower classes. There were many such people about, well-dressed and articulate socialists who harangued the workers with the need for social change and then, their socialist duty done, retired to comfortable quarters and full plates, leaving their audiences to be nourished by ideas. Orwell managed to convince most of those he met of his own sincerity, although his determination to stay occasionally in quarters few workers would visit gave some of the people he interviewed a bit of concern. It would not do for him to show workers living with slop jars by their feet as they ate.

In Wigan, Orwell observed the workers close up, watching as they met and argued politics, speaking with their wives about domestic conditions, asking questions, taking notes. Trains bearing mountainous loads of refuse and dirt often passed through Wigan, and the unemployed workers leaped onto the cars, shovels in hand, pushing heaps of trash onto the sides of the tracks in hopes of finding a lump or two of coal among the debris. They had no food, they had no heat, they had little hope.

Orwell spent a good deal of his time in the Wigan library, a gathering place for many workers. As Orwell proceeded diligently to unearth facts and figures for his book, he became aware that the people in the library were not there in search of education or information. It was a public building open to them and it was warm. Their anger seethed, but with many it did little good to talk about the future: how could one worry about the future when uncertain of how to get through a single day? Orwell continued to make notes.

Late in February Orwell took his first journey down into a coal mine. He wanted to witness firsthand the conditions endured by those still employed. He traveled nine hundred feet down into cramped tunnels. His height was a problem. Even men of average height had to stoop as they made their way through the mines; Orwell found himself bent nearly double for long hours. He cracked his head repeatedly on the timbers with which the mine was shored up. It was a filthy, dark, claustrophobic world, as empty of hope in its own way as was the world of the unemployed above.

By March 1936, the expedition to Wigan had taken its toll on Orwell's health. He went to Liverpool, but his strength gave out there, and he was cared for by a socialist couple to whom he presented a letter of introduction even as he collapsed. He remained in bed for only a few days, however, rising to go to Sheffield for an examination of the conditions there. Sheffield was in coal-mining territory, but its industrial base was more diversified than that of Wigan. Textile and other unemployed factory workers were little different from shipyard workers or miners. They had all experienced the theft of their future, and more than a few felt that a new future must be created from political and social revolution. Reform was not enough.

Orwell stayed in Sheffield with a communist whose works had appeared occasionally in the *Adelphi*, but who was now too caught up in the idea of communism and Marxist theory to write. Orwell listened patiently as the wonders of Marxism were explained, and endured a bit of jibing about his own middle-class background. He left Sheffield soon to revisit his own family, staying for a time with his sister Marjorie and her husband, first in their home in Bristol, then briefly at their country cottage. When he left Marjorie he returned to the mines again, but this time he was better prepared. He visited newer mines as well, better lighted, seemingly safer than the older ones. The system, though, that operated those mines, and condemned men to a life in them, continued to prey upon Orwell's thoughts. He began seeking in earnest for a form for his book.

His journey to the north was nearly over. Orwell had begun the trip as a writer on assignment, a novelist taking a journalistic sabbatical. He had carried with him the galleys of *Keep the Aspidistra Flying*, and, early on in his trip, would spend evenings going over the novel after a long day of social and political investigation. The novel had been altered somewhat because Gollancz again feared a libel suit. But the changes bothered Orwell less than the narrowness of the book's point of view. Gordon Comstock was no artist, no revolutionary, no thinker. He was of the middle class and only pretended to those things; the same charges had been leveled at his creator by unemployed people and by working-class political activists. Orwell returned the corrected proofs to Gollancz, but he was enormously dissatisfied with the novel, both as a piece of art and as a piece of politics. He'd turned inward too long, concentrating on character rather than culture, psychology rather than society. He would change that with the new book, if he could find the right approach to his materials.

Before returning home he attended another political gathering. Orwell had listened to communists, to socialists, to ministers of various religions, to the ILP, the NUWM, to organizations whose names were not worth noting. In mid-March he attended a rally held by Oswald Mosley, who'd broken with the

Labour Party at the beginning of the 1930s and had formed an organization called the British Union of Fascists. Mosley's followers wore black shirts as symbols of their fascism, and cheered their leader as he called for a revolution of his own. Those in the audience who dissented were beaten. It was not only the left that sought support in those trying times.

By April 1936, Orwell was finished and returned to the south. Although he went briefly to London, he had no intention of staying there, or in any city. He had had enough of cities. Cities and their demands—for food, for fuel, for raw materials— had played too large a part in creating the problem's he'd just seen. Orwell was ready to move to the country, and to settle there with Eileen if he could find a place they could afford. He wanted the tranquility of rural life as he thought and worked his way through the political ideas that would form the heart of the book Gollancz had commissioned. Through friends he heard of a likely spot, Wallington, and he traveled there to see the house they had found.

Wallington, with barely two hundred people, sounded like the sort of village he'd hoped for, the sort in which, had his choices been different, he might have become a vicar and led a quiet, perhaps scholarly life. He left the main highway between London and Cambridge and still had a few miles of narrow lanes to cover before he found the house he was to rent. It had once been a crossroads store, he knew, and one of its appeals was the thought of reopening the store for business and perhaps generating a bit of extra income. He had been told that the house was small.

When he finally arrived in Wallington, Orwell was enchanted to discover just how small the house really was. A child would not have thought it large. The Stores, as it was called, was not quite two dozen feet long, less than half that wide. There were two rooms on the ground floor, each eleven by eleven feet, a tiny kitchen, and two bedrooms upstairs. The Stores was almost too small even to be called a cottage, and Orwell banged his head on the low ceilings. He had stayed in lodging houses where the rooms were larger. But The Stores was no lodging, it was a home, and its small size gave him a sense of security, not claustrophobia. He signed a lease for the house and immediately set to work clearing a garden and building a chicken house. If he was going to live in the country, he was going to raise vegetables and keep animals. He pruned the fruit trees, and soon had chickens, geese, and goats to keep him company.

Eileen would be with him before the summer ended: they planned to marry in early June. First, Orwell had to prepare The Stores for occupancy, as well as do the preparatory work required for his new book. *Keep the Aspidistra Flying* was published on April 20, 1936, in an edition of 3,000 copies; it did not find an American publisher, and the British edition sold only moderately. He told any who inquired that he did not care for the novel, and that he was taking a break from novel writing. He felt his novels to be too shallow, lacking commitment, or insight, or something. It was the writer's responsibility, Orwell felt with increasing passion, to use his abilities to tell the truth. He had tried throughout his career to do that, but after Wigan he realized that narrow novelistic truth was no longer sufficient for his purposes or ambitions. He was looking for more.

Although temporarily off novels, Orwell returned to the essay in late May at the request of the editor of *New Writing*. With all the details of The Stores to attend to, the looming marriage, the new book, Orwell felt obliged to describe the planned piece first, in a letter, as a way of determining editorial interest. The editor encouraged Orwell to proceed with the essay, one of his reminiscences of Burma, an account of the execution of an elephant.

An elephant had gone on a rampage and killed a Burmese. Orwell, as he re-created the story in the essay, was summoned to kill the elephant. But the rampage was ended, the animal docile. Orwell decided not to kill it. A crowd of Burmese had gathered, though, staring at the young police officer in his uniform. The situation, as recalled in the essay, became more clear.

"And suddenly I realised that I should have to shoot the elephant after all. The people expected it of me and I had to do it; I could feel their two thousand wills pressing me forward, irresistibly. And it was at this moment, as I stood there with the rifle in my hands, that I first grasped the hollowness, the futility of the white man's dominion in the East. Here was I, the white man with his gun, standing in front of the unarmed native crowd—seemingly the leading actor of the piece; but in reality I was only an absurd puppet pushed to and fro by the will of those yellow faces behind. I perceived in this moment that when the white man turns tyrant it is his own freedom that he destroys."

He understood that if he did not kill the elephant he would be laughed at, and from the vantage point of his typewriter he understood that the one thing tyrants can never endure is being laughed at. The elephant fell to the young officer's gun, and the young officer avoided the overwhelming catastrophe of appearing foolish before the empire's subjects. Orwell called the piece "Shooting an Elephant" and it appeared in the fall of 1936.

His experiences in Burma were one thing to write about: they had been filtered now through a decade of experience and hindsight. In "Shooting an Elephant" Orwell wrote as a mature man, his insights fully formed. The experiences in the industrial north, in Wigan and Sheffield, were more difficult to put into words. They were too fresh. Orwell had written his notes up once as a diary, but he remained dissatisfied. There was politics in the story he had been assigned to write, and facts and figures to document the politics, but there was also human drama; there were ideas, but there were also emotions to be described. He had to make readers feel the drama if he was to persuade them of the politics.

In June, as he worked and reworked the opening portions of his manuscript, Orwell married Eileen O'Shaughnessy, bringing a certain order to his domestic life at least. The wedding was small and took place on June 9, 1936. Before the ceremony Eileen was drawn aside by both Ida and Avril Blair, and advised that she was entering into marriage with a man of limited responsibility. Eileen did not mind, and did not particularly believe the criticism. Orwell knew his family considered him eccentric. The couple settled into The Stores, and soon established a comfortable and productive routine. Eileen was by no means a quiet and traditional homemaker—her political attitudes differed in some particulars from her husband's, and she did not shrink from giving him fiery argument. However, she rose early to prepare a large breakfast for the two of them. She told her friends that if she did not attend to such details Orwell would simply forget to eat, spending all of his time sitting at the typewriter, smoking cigarettes, and drinking strong tea.

Most of Orwell's time that summer of 1936 was spent at his machine, or working on The Stores. The garden had fallen into disrepair, it was thick with weeds, but Orwell continued to work daily at clearing it. He and Eileen began learning the intricacies of operating their small shop, attempting to gauge the market for different products, remaining alert to inventory, keeping the books. Most of their customers were children, spending their pennies on candy. Orwell and Eileen had discussed having children of their own, but by their first anniversary it became clear that conception would not come easily, if at all. They spoke of the possibility of adoption, but decided to wait. Perhaps the problem was a temporary one.

Occasionally friends would make the journey from London to visit the couple in their tiny cottage. The ILP offered a series of summer lectures, a sort of political school, in nearby Letchworth, and Orwell attended several sessions there, arguing dogma with other left-wing political writers and activists. He gave several lectures himself that summer, and in book reviews increasingly focused upon political themes. His Wigan book was at last beginning to take shape, and as it did Orwell's political thoughts grew more clear. He enjoyed a correspondence with the American novelist Henry Miller, whose *Tropic of Cancer* had broken ground in its frank presentation of sexuality and natural life. Miller, who greatly admired the honesty and clarity of Orwell's work, advised him to abandon politics as a theme and more fully embrace life itself. But Orwell was lost in politics and would not listen.

As his book on British unemployment and politics took shape, Orwell's attention was split. He argued in his book that a political revolution would be required in Britain before there was any sort of economic justice, but as his book neared its second half he began to realize that none of the factions seeking the support of the unemployed were adequate to the task of reforming the economic situation. The ILP, the NUWM, the communists, the socialists—each group was so caught up in the details of its own dogma and internal debate that it lost sight of the purposes to which it supposedly devoted itself. Some leaders became obsessed with power for its own sake, others— especially the socialists—cost themselves support by their own eccentricity. ". . . there is the horrible—the really disquieting— prevalence of cranks wherever Socialists are gathered together. One sometimes gets the impression that the mere words Socialism and Communism draw towards them with magnetic force every fruit-juice drinker, nudist, sandal-wearer, sex-maniac, Quaker, Nature Cure quack, pacifist and feminist in England." Orwell painted a portrait of socialism as the commonsense solution to Britain's problems, but also an acid picture of socialists, mostly from the middle classes, whose interest in the political movement was prompted either by eccentricity or, oddly, by their own sense of "social prestige." His prose was clear and his arguments well made, but even as he wrote he knew that Victor Gollancz would not be pleased with the book produced as a result of his assignment.

While taking British socialists to task, Orwell was captivated by the socialist movement under way in Spain. By late in the summer of 1936, Spain was divided into armed camps, workers with weapons attempting to fight back against the military's seizure of the Spanish government. The battle lines in Spain were political as well as geographic and strategic: the left, with communists, socialists, and a variety of revolutionaries fighting side by side against the fascists. Left-wing thinkers around the world began to rally to the cause of the Spanish left, and volunteers from many different countries traveled to Spain. The fascists, led by Francisco Franco, had begun receiving the support of the German leader, Adolf Hitler, and the Italian leader, Benito Mussolini. Orwell himself gave thought to traveling to Spain, to put his life on the line where before he had only put words. In Spain there was a war going on for control of a nation.

Words were his occupation, however, and throughout the fall as Spain's conflict grew increasingly bloody, Orwell labored to complete his manuscript. He called the book *The Road to Wigan Pier*, taking its title from his attempt to visit a famous pier, only to find that it was long destroyed. The book's final shape, divided into two parts of roughly equal size, prompted Gollancz to suggest separate publication of the halves. The first half, a documentary of Orwell's journey, was a gray and moving portrait of the despair of the unemployed, beginning with a horrifying scene of degradation. It was the sort of book Orwell was known for, supported with facts and figures as well as anecdotes and incidents.

It was *The Road to Wigan Pier*'s second half that proved problematical to Gollancz, as Orwell had anticipated. Gollancz had his reputation as a left-wing thinker and publisher to consider, and Orwell's criticisms of the people on the left were too acute, too offensive. Orwell, though, would not permit the book to be divided. He stood by what he wrote, and in late 1936 Gollancz resigned himself to publishing the book as a whole. It would be a unique whole, however, for Gollancz felt impelled to write a long introduction to Orwell's text. This apologia made clear Gollancz's admiration for the first half of the book, but made clear also that the publisher felt the second half to be the work of a man as eccentric as the socialist characters pictured in the book. Certainly Orwell was sincere, Gollancz felt, but he was also naive and politically unschooled; Orwell's portrait of Soviet communism as being equally rapacious and mechanical as the worst of capitalism, was, according to Gollancz, simply wrong.

Despite his reservations, Gollancz made *The Road to Wigan Pier* a major offering of his firm's Left Book Club, and quickly sold more than 40,000 copies, with a second and then a third printing ordered. The trade edition appeared in March 1937, and sold fewer than 2,000 copies. And, to get at least a bit more of his own way, Gollancz also published a separate edition of the first section of the book, recommending that activists on the left use it as a means of recruiting more people to their cause.

By the time *The Road to Wigan Pier* was published, its author had been in Spain for three months. He'd made up his mind to join the fight, and by winter 1936 his plans were taking shape. As was Orwell's custom, he obtained letters of introduction to people whom it might be valuable to know. He helped Eileen prepare The Stores for operation without him. He dealt with a variety of literary details, and by December was on his way to the Spanish front. He stopped briefly in Paris and visited Henry Miller, who remained convinced that Orwell was risking his life for no good reason, but nonetheless provided him with a warm corduroy coat. The day after Christmas 1936, George Orwell arrived in Barcelona.

Britain's industrial north had impressed Orwell with its widespread despair, but Barcelona was alive with the unity of spirit that, he'd always known, would accompany true revolution. Everyone was an equal, a comrade. The workers ran every aspect of the city; even barbers spoke of revolution as they clipped hair. This was the future, the way things should be, like-minded people standing shoulder to shoulder. They might be undersupplied and underfed, but they were equals facing up to the threat of fascism. Orwell had told his friends that he was going to Spain as a journalist, but once he arrived he knew that he would have to fight. He had been an observer too long, he wanted now to share the struggle.

He made his way to the Barcelona office of the ILP and presented his letters of introduction. It did not take long for Orwell to learn that, despite the surface appearance of unity of purpose, Spain's noble resistance was as segmented and factionalized as the left wing in Britain. The ILP supported the United Marxist Workers' Party, called POUM after its Spanish initials (Partido Obrero de Unificación Marxista), a group that fielded a militia and fought bravely against the fascists. But the POUM was viewed with some suspicion by the communists, whose support went to the Unión General de Trabajadores (UGT), a Spanish trade union organization. The Soviet Union was providing arms, equipment, and financial aid to the Spanish revolutionaries, but was also wary of the POUM. The communists considered the POUM dangerously allied to Lev Davidovich Trotsky, who had been expelled from the Soviet communist party and deported from Russia in the late 1920s. Trotsky's fall had resulted from the same sort of party fragmentation that Orwell began to perceive in Spain. Soviet Marxists wanted their revolution their way and would tolerate no deviation from the principles of communism as they saw them. Trotskyite sympathizers were seen as traitors to the cause, and in Spain there was a gathering tension between the groups.

Political sensibilities and sympathies aside, Orwell brought one skill to Spain that earned him a warm welcome: he could, as a result of his training in Burma, handle a rifle. For a group of revolutionaries involved in a desperate war there was, to Orwell, a shocking lack of military experience, skill, and discipline. He enlisted almost upon arrival in the POUM militia, was issued one of the few rifles available, and set to work as a drill instructor, seeking to instill some sense of military efficiency and order in the men with whom he served. It was not easy. Orwell's rifle was older than the century, and it was virtually the only weapon among a training group of fifty men. Orwell patiently showed the others how to break down the rifle, clean it, and reassemble it. They practiced firing the rifle, but not often, for there was little ammunition, and frequently it was the wrong size. For their part, the militiamen endeavored to get Orwell drunk. They failed, and he was accepted as a comrade in arms. The speed with which he mastered Spanish also impressed them.

Early in 1937 Orwell traveled to the front, joining POUM militiamen in Catalonia in northeast Spain. He encamped with young Spanish union workers and several dozen British volunteers who had joined through the ILP. Orwell at thirty-three was older than many of the Spanish, and he brought a certain commonsense approach to the business of war. At the time, fighting was sporadic in Catalonia, with most of the conflict consisting of sniper duels. When food was in short supply Orwell would find the nearest source, in more than one case a field of potatoes. He would measure the distance between the field and the nearest fascist emplacement and calculate the range of the enemy weapons. If their weapons lacked the range needed to hit him, he would calmly set forth for the harvest while his companions urged him to behave more sensibly. Orwell maintained that his behavior was above all sensible, and they all dined on fresh potatoes. The other members of the militia marveled at his coolness almost as much as they marveled at the sight of his feet: some claimed that Orwell's boots were the largest they had ever seen.

He settled into the routine of war easily, keeping mainly to himself, writing letters to Eileen, joining in the infrequent action. Orwell developed a more clear understanding of the POUM position, sympathizing with POUM members over their opposition to the centralization that was a hallmark of Soviet communism. The POUM argued with increasing fire that the Spanish Civil War should be seized as an opportunity for a workers' revolt, that it was a war of true revolution as well as a war against the fascists. The results of such a revolution would be not only the defeat of fascism, but also the creation of a new form of government, a more equitable form, for all of Spain. The communists, increasingly influenced by Stalin and advisers from Russia, disagreed: the war was against fascism alone. Once won, said the communists, the central government would be restored, doubtless with a strong Stalinist slant. As spring deepened, so did the sense of distrust between the two factions.

Eileen arrived in Spain in February, bringing cigars and other items for her husband. They managed to meet occasionally throughout the spring, and Orwell revealed that he was giving some thought to leaving the POUM and joining the more closely communist-affiliated International Brigade in Madrid. Perhaps he wanted to spend time with the other side, having absorbed the arguments of the POUM members and the anarchists. But this shift was not to be. By May the tension between the POUM and the communists erupted into a bloody conflict, a civil war within a civil war. The communists charged that the POUM was operating under false pretenses, that it was actually composed of fascists, and that it received aid and equipment from the fascists. The communist propaganda machine unleashed its efforts to brand all of the noncommunist revolutionaries in Spain as tools of the Germans and the Italians, betrayers of the Marxist cause. The power of print became clear to Orwell: what the communists wrote appeared in black and white and it mattered little that none of it was true. It was in print and it sounded like the truth, and to many readers it simply became the truth. Barricades sprouted throughout Barcelona, windows were shuttered, gunfire was exchanged between former comrades: hundreds died, more than a thousand were wounded.

Late in May, bitter at the turn of events, Orwell returned to the front to serve as an officer with an ILP unit in the trenches. Orwell was taller than the trenches were deep, but his disregard for danger, along with his dislike for bending over or crouching, kept his head high above the lip of the trench. He was standing tall, telling stories, early on the morning of May 20 when a sniper's bullet finally found him, entering his throat below the larynx and passing out the back.

The bullet had found Orwell but it had fortunately missed his spinal cord. He was lucky as well that the fascists possessed more modern weapons than the revolutionaries. The high speed of the modern rifle with which he was shot served to generate great heat, which sealed the wound as the bullet passed through. It looked for a while, though, as if he would die, and at best that he would never speak again. He was transferred from a field hospital to a more modern facility, and then to Barcelona. Eileen joined him, staying by his side as he regained his strength, and more slowly, the use of his voice. His speech was hoarse, his voice lower than it had been, but he was gradually able to form words, to make himself understood. He lay in his hospital bed alongside other wounded volunteers, and in early June he returned to the front and requested a medical discharge from the militia. The discharge was approved, and by the middle of the month Orwell was on his way to Barcelona, where he would rejoin Eileen and make his way back to Britain.

The conflict between the communists and the POUM had changed its tenor as Orwell recuperated. The initial round of fighting between the groups had ended, and the communists, through the police they controlled, had begun a purge of the revolutionaries, arresting as many of them as they could find. Membership in the POUM, the ILP, or the Anarchist Party was now a criminal offense. Men beside whom Orwell had fought for a cause were now jailed with little pretense of due process, and Spaniards and foreign volunteers alike were locked up indiscriminately. Eileen had been confronted one night by a police contingent come without warning to search her hotel room. She had managed to hide the incriminating documents she carried, and when Orwell arrived in Barcelona she advised him to go into hiding as well. He slept with other fugitives in shattered buildings, still weak from his wounds but strengthened by the bitterness that flowed through him. This was no revolution. It was a situation as totalitarian in its denial of any freedom of dissent as that of the fascists. Late in June he and Eileen made their way into France, fearing that at any moment they, too, would be rounded up.

Despite his wound, despite the paranoia which had drained him and Eileen as they escaped from Spain, despite his exhaustion, Orwell could not wait to get to his typewriter. If the communists could use words, so could he. He barely took the time to catch his breath after arriving at The Stores in early July before sitting at his desk and beginning work on a long article about the Spanish dilemma. He had cabled from France a description of the article to the editor of *New English Weekly;* the request for the piece was at The Stores waiting for him. Orwell called the article "Spilling the Spanish Beans" and despite the speed of its composition it was clearly written. Orwell's anger was held in check: it would do no good to froth at the mouth, or on the page. He sought to tell the truth as he had seen it, and he made obvious from his opening paragraphs that there was a reign of terror taking place in Spain at the communists' direction. He also emphasized that the communist press was manipulating the world's left-wing readers, using their fear of fascism as a means of distracting them from the horrors the communists themselves were committing.

The piece was rejected by the editor who had requested it. Once again Orwell discovered the difficulty involved in saying anything critical of the communists in Britain's left-wing press. "Spilling the Spanish Beans" eventually found a magazine willing to print it, but throughout the late summer of 1937 Orwell found his writings about Spain going homeless. Book reviews were rejected on the grounds that they disagreed too overtly with the positions presented by the communists, not because what Orwell said was untrue. Orwell continued to write, launching himself into a book-length treatment of Spain even as his shorter pieces were, if not suppressed, at least ignored. He also found himself under attack for the views expressed in *The Road to Wigan Pier,* with the British communist reviewers particularly harsh in their criticisms. They branded him a snob, a middle-class writer whose contempt for the poor and their smells, they claimed, showed through on every page. Orwell remained at The Stores, helping Eileen with the management of the shop and the garden, but spending most of his time at the typewriter, building a portrait of the Spanish Civil War and the part he had played in it.

He completed the new book early in 1938. Orwell experienced none of the difficulties of composition with *Homage to Catalonia,* as he called the new manuscript, that he had with *The Road to Wigan Pier.* In the earlier book he had attempted to describe the perils of factionalism among the left; now he wrote of the consequences of those perils. He realized that the communists could be even more extreme in their actions than the fascists—more totalitarian, more fearful of any original thought, more willing to go to any extreme to crush dissidents and revolutionaries. Theirs were crimes of calculation, but according to Orwell the left in Britain shared complicity because they simply ignored the communist purges. If Orwell needed further evidence he had received it early in the book's composition, when Gollancz suggested, before Orwell was more than a few pages into the manuscript, that Orwell should take it to another publisher. The communists labeled the POUM fascists, and as a publisher Gollancz would have nothing to do with a book that dealt favorably with fascists.

Orwell's new publishers, Secker and Warburg, proved more than willing to let Orwell express his own views. Fredric Warburg, one of the company's principals, was closely allied to the ILP, and other ILP members were constantly requesting that Orwell join their cause. As publication of his new book neared, Orwell found himself increasingly drawn to the ILP. He still had some hope that in Britain at least independent socialist organizations such as the ILP could bring about a revolution and avoid the terrible pogroms that accompanied communist takeovers. His hope, though, was tempered by his common sense and his understanding of political reality. *Homage to Catalonia* presented the story of revolutionary ideals compromised and finally crushed or consumed by the forces that dwelled within the revolutionaries themselves. Orwell had concluded the book with an account of his and Eileen's flight from Spain, building to a final paragraph in which he returned to the land of his birth. The British seemed so removed from everything.

"Earthquakes in Japan, famines in China, revolutions in Mexico? Don't worry, the milk will be on the doorstep tomorrow morning, the *New Statesman* will come out on Friday. The industrial towns were far away, a smudge of smoke and misery hidden by the curve of the earth's surface. Down here it was still the England I had known in my childhood: the railway cuttings smothered in wild flowers, the deep meadows where the great shining horses browse and meditate, the slow-moving streams bordered by willows, the green bosoms of the elms, the larkspurs in the cottage gardens; and then the huge peaceful wilderness of outer London, the barges on the miry river, the familiar streets, the posters telling of cricket matches and Royal weddings, the men in bowler hats, the pigeons in Trafalgar Square, the red buses, the blue policemen—all sleeping the deep, deep sleep of England, from which I sometimes fear that we shall never wake till we are jerked out of it by the roar of bombs."

Orwell knew what was coming, had seen in Spain only a rehearsal for the conflagration that would envelop the world before too many more years had passed. He had experienced and been outraged by the subversion of principle to the ends of political expediency, and had come to view Soviet communism as an evil growth against which people of integrity must stand up. His revulsion did not drive him back to capitalism; Orwell returned from Spain more completely committed to socialism than ever. In Spain he had also seen the face of war, had been wounded himself, and lain with the wounded. He had also killed, but at a distance, with hand grenades. In *Homage to Catalonia* he told a story of once getting a fascist soldier in the sights of his rifle, only to realize that the enemy had his pants around his ankles and was involved with a simple, universal, nonpolitical need. He brought home with him the truth that people going to the bathroom were not the enemy, but only people, as well as the truth that not every ally should be openly embraced. *Homage to Catalonia* was in many ways Orwell's first great book: he had arrived at a complex political position, but had learned to express that position with clarity and simplicity. Soon, he knew, bombs would rain on everyone, and everyone would be politicized. But everyone would also be, simultaneously, in the position of the fascist Orwell had been unable to shoot: common people, neither good nor bad, placed in situations of danger and subject to manipulation. His account of Spain was his sixth book, but he felt himself only just beginning to get to work.

EIGHT

BROADCASTING THROUGH THE BLITZ

ORWELL'S HEALTH KEPT HIM from getting on too quickly with the work he so desperately wanted to do. In early March 1938, he began bleeding from the left lung. Evidently he'd had a mild case of tuberculosis when younger, and one of the lesions left by the disease was acting up. Orwell found himself committed to a sanatorium, along with other lung patients seeking a clean climate and fresh air for their health. The only activity he was permitted was an occasional afternoon of fishing; his doctors forbade the use of a typewriter or even pen and paper for more than a few hours a week. He was able only to write book reviews, but he took his confinement as an opportunity to consider the format of his next book. He'd written two nonfiction works and was ready to return to the novel, but he wanted his new novel to carry greater political content than his previous one. The introspection of Gordon Comstock in *Keep the Aspidistra Flying* must be replaced by something larger, more reflective of his own enlarged consciousness.

Homage to Catalonia was published by Secker and Warburg late in April, while its author remained on his back in a hospital bed. Any apprehensions Orwell may have felt about having so controversial a book published while he was too ill to respond to criticisms quickly evaporated. It became clear soon after publication that *Homage to Catalonia* was going to be denied a great deal of attention. Secker and Warburg believed in the value of the book, but they also knew the effect that a large controversy would have on sales: people flocked to purchase controversial books. Attacks from the left would only boost the success of *Homage to Catalonia.*

The controversy failed to materialize. The left was more dismissive of the book, at least in print, than publicly angered by it. Many of the reviews took the tone of steering readers away from a book about the United Marxist Workers' Party (POUM), the Trotskyites who were enemies of the Spanish left. Orwell's prose received favorable notice but his politics were sneered at. The communists had revealed the complicity of the POUM, and any apologia for the traitors would find little welcome among the left-wing reviewers in Britain. They knew the truth because they had read it in the communist and left-wing papers. Orwell responded to one column which had charged that the POUM was directly under the control of Franco, but other than that there was little for him to do. Secker and Warburg printed a first edition of 1,500 copies; it proved far more than were needed to meet the demand. It would be fifteen years before an American edition appeared. It was a reaction to which Orwell was accustomed: one more of his works was being ignored.

In the sanatorium Orwell made notes for his new novel, worked at an idea for an antiwar pamphlet, gave thought to politics and his own political ideas. Eileen could make the trip to visit him only twice a month, having to spend most of her time in Wallington minding The Stores. Orwell got along well with the other patients, mostly ex-servicemen, and divided his time between conversations with them and solitary stints either fishing or in his room. He followed the news of the Spanish Civil War, reading the reports of the increased German and Italian presence in the conflict, watching the reports carefully as the fascists unleashed the power of modern mechanized air warfare. War, with bombs raining on the British countryside, could not be far off now. Orwell, for his part, joined the ILP officially, taking a stand with his membership as he had with his type-writer.

By August he had recuperated sufficiently for his doctors to begin discussing discharge. They recommended strongly that he and Eileen go to a warm climate for the winter, but money, as always for Orwell, remained a problem. The failure of *Homage to Catalonia* to sell had been a serious setback, and the income from reviews was a mere trickle. The Stores generated more expenses than it did income, despite Eileen's careful manage-ment of the shop. Orwell cut back on his smoking, steeling himself for another English winter. L. H. Myers, a novelist who had enjoyed some success with a quartet of novels about India, learned of Orwell's plight. An admirer of Orwell's work, Myers put up £300, anonymously, to finance a season in Morocco for Orwell and Eileen.

They arrived in Marrakesh in September 1938, and stayed in a hotel until they found a small villa they could afford. Typi-cally for Orwell, his first acts upon settling into the new home were to obtain a few small animals—chickens and a goat—and some vegetable seeds. He might by his health be exiled from The Stores, but he would not give up his gardening. As always he and Eileen gave names to the animals, making up little stories about them from time to time.

Orwell also struck up a correspondence with ILP members he knew who could provide him with special knowledge about the insurance industry and the life of insurance salesmen. He was beginning to develop the characterization of his new novel's protagonist. He would make the character, George Dowling, an insurance salesman, a man whose products were purchased by people fearful of the future, and whose employers generated profits by being statistically optimistic about the future. Dowl-ing, as he began to come to life on the page, was caught some-where between optimism and pessimism, a man of middle years who takes a journey back to the cherished spots of his youth only to find them destroyed by urban sprawl and technological progress. Orwell called the novel *Coming Up for Air*. He completed the first draft before New Year 1939.

As Orwell revised his novel in the opening months of the new year, Dowling's fears about the future, about bombed-out London streets, about the spread of sloganeering and official control of society, were mirrored in Spain. Barcelona fell on January 26, 1939, and by late March Madrid had fallen. The opening battle of the war had ended in a fascist victory. But *Coming Up for Air* had, beneath its surface of grime and pollution and political fear, a current of optimism, just as in the novel cleaner currents would flow through the polluted streams that so depressed Dowling. The middle class, Orwell said with this novel, the decent and ordinary men and women of Britain had it within them to effect the changes that were required to make the world livable once more. By April Orwell and Eileen were back home from Morocco and the new novel had been delivered to Gollancz. At the same time, German troops were marching into Czechoslovakia, with Hitler announcing to the world that they had been invited in by the Czech government.

As Gollancz readied *Coming Up for Air* for the printers, Orwell returned to The Stores and set to work clearing the garden. He did not feel up to another novel immediately, and instead turned his attention to the compilation of a book of essays. Late in June he traveled to Southwold on a summons from his family: Richard Blair had cancer and the end was near. Orwell's father died on June 28, 1939, with his son sitting nearby. The long life of the opium officer who so believed in empire had ended. His son's latest novel had sold more than 2,000 copies that month, its first in print. Orwell returned to The Stores after the funeral. His relationship with his father had never been close, but the two had loved each other. Orwell missed Richard Blair's solidity.

Coming Up for Air began with brisk sales, requiring an almost immediate second printing, but soon slowed. Orwell concentrated upon his collection of essays and a variety of antiwar writings. He wanted to make clear that unless the coming war was fought as an antiimperialist war, a war not only against the imperialism as practiced by the fascists but also against Britain and France's own imperialist tendencies, it would not be worth fighting. He passed his time writing and raising flowers, formulating his antiwar ideas. The arguments he constructed that summer collapsed in August when, in a stunning surprise, Stalin and Hitler announced a nonaggression treaty. Within weeks Soviet troops were fighting alongside Nazis in the subjugation of Poland. The communist press, of course, defended the pact, and with those words sought to create their own reality. Many of Orwell's friends resigned from the communist party, but many ILP members remained willing to argue that the coming war was a war against capitalism solely, that communism was still acceptable. Orwell left the ILP. On September 3, 1939, Great Britain and France declared war on Germany. Orwell began rethinking his arguments.

He would not surrender his opposition to capitalism and his hatred of empire. Capitalism and imperialism were at the root of the conflict that was erupting. But Britain, whose empire spanned the world and whose economy was capitalist, was also a democracy, populated by people not unlike George Dowling of *Coming Up for Air* or George Orwell, its author. Their decency could be appealed to, even as their patriotism and detestation of totalitarianism led them to join the effort against the Axis. Orwell was ready to do his bit, but had first to determine what that bit would be.

Eileen found her path more quickly than did her husband. Before the war was a month old she had left The Stores and moved to London, finding a job with, ironically, the government's Censorship Department. Orwell remained at the cottage, tending the animals and the garden, selling candy to children, and completing his book of essays. He finished the manuscript by the end of the year, calling the book *Inside the Whale* after one of the essays it contained. They were literary essays mainly, but they were political as well. "Inside the Whale" itself began as a discussion of Henry Miller's *Tropic of Cancer* but built into a long rumination on the political nature underlying modern literature. A piece on "Boys' Weeklies" examined the pulp stories he recalled so fondly from his youth, and at the same time examined themes, political and social, that ran throughout popular literature. His mastery of the essay form was complete, and he allowed his pieces now to find their own length as he worked his way through his arguments.

Orwell was attempting to find work of another sort, busily writing letters seeking some sort of job where he could help the war effort. He was not quite sure what he wanted to do, or what could be done with him. For a time he thought that his fondness for fiddling with equipment might lead him into mechanical draftsmanship, but nothing came of that. His health kept him from working in one of the ministries. Orwell thought that his writings were an aid to the war effort, at least an aid in presenting a divergent point of view to those who read his books, but readership remained small. Gollancz had felt *Inside the Whale*'s prospects sufficiently poor to offer only a £20 advance. During wartime it seemed unlikely that people would come out in great numbers for a volume of essays, no matter how masterful, that revealed the hidden political nature of works such as those of Dickens. The book met Gollancz's expectations.

By the time *Inside the Whale* appeared in March 1940, Orwell was preparing to leave the gentle countryside and Wallington and The Stores where he had been so happy. Although he kept the lease, he sold off his livestock and moved to London in May, joining Eileen in a dreary small apartment. His work was dreary as well. While Orwell wanted to undertake a truly ambitious novel, one that might span several generations and several volumes, he found himself reviewing plays and movies for *Time and Tide*, an undistinguished journal that had no real political force or stance. Orwell loathed the work, but he and Eileen needed even the small amount that his reviews brought in. He did no work on the novel. On several occasions he attempted to enlist in the Army, but he continued to be turned down. He joined the Home Guard, a militia formed for the defense of Britain, and became a sergeant of "C" Company of the County of London's Fifth Home Guard Battalion. Orwell realized that the Soviet Union could not arm its private citizens, nor could any totalitarian state: the risk of armed revolt was too great. In Britain the common people took their arms and their domestic defense responsibilities seriously, and unified their purpose with that expressed by the government: the nation must be defended, the fascists defeated. Orwell encouraged other socialists to join the Home Guard, not to spark revolution, but to stand as good common people alongside other good common people, to demonstrate that socialists were not to be feared, and that revolutionaries could be as patriotic as the next person.

Patriotism was much on his mind. Orwell approached the nature of patriotism and its relation to his own political ideas from several directions. In an article called "Wells, Hitler and the World State" he acknowledged the great influence of H. G. Wells's ideas and works on himself and his generation. But, he argued, Wells had lost touch with reality, and become too caught up in the *idea* of a World State with one unified government. Patriotism, Orwell said, got in the way of such a government coming about. Wells failed to take simple, common patriotism into account and that was why his books remained structures simply of ideas and had no significant effect upon society.

Orwell spoke of the great attraction of military precision, and he was attracted to it himself, priding himself upon the discipline he brought to his Company "C" responsibilities. He did not forget his socialism, and constantly made the point that an armed working class was a great symbol of democracy. At the same time, he made notes for a project about urban warfare, whether for defense against invasion or revolt against oppression. Toward the end of summer he undertook one of the longest essays of his career, *The Lion and the Unicorn.* The essay was to serve as the first pamphlet in a series called The Searchlight Books, to be published by Secker and Warburg. Orwell played a part in the development of the books, serving as one of the series' editors. Authors were to be given complete freedom in their choice of a subject and the approach they took to it. The series was intended to aid the war effort and also to recommend or advocate reforms that would improve the postwar world.

Orwell wrote *The Lion and the Unicorn* in just a few months, but he had spent years considering its subject. He wrote of the British people, their peculiar natures, their eccentricities, and the ability of adversity to change eccentricity into virtue. In times of crisis all British people pulled as one. Their patriotism lay beneath the surface, a private matter, until threatened. Patriotism, Orwell had come to realize, could form the core of a workable socialism. In Germany, in all of the totalitarian countries, patriotism had been poisoned, but in Britain it could not be. British patriotism could not be roused by cries for conquest: only by the need for defense. The British had acquired an empire more than they had conquered one, and its acquisition had been by virtue of a navy rather than a large army. The government's request for Home Guard volunteers brought more than two hundred and fifty thousand volunteers the first day, but in peacetime Britain had trouble keeping even a small army. England's immunity rested upon a commonsense decency.

Orwell's insight and prose were up to the ambition of the essay. Everything came together at his typewriter as he smoked cigarette after cigarette, rolling the rough tobacco in a little machine. "A military parade," he wrote, "is really a kind of ritual dance, something like a ballet, expressing a certain philosophy of life. The goose-step, for instance, is one of the most horrible sights in the world, far more terrifying than a dive bomber. It is simply an affirmation of naked power; contained in it, quite consciously and intentionally, is the vision of a boot crashing down on a face." He captured totalitarianism by chilling his readers, then thawing them with his common sense. "Why is the goose-step not used in England? . . . It is not used because the people in the street would laugh." The pamphlet was a masterpiece of polemical writing, frightening and witty, criticizing and advocating, visionary and yet sound. Orwell envisioned a planned Britain, a socialist Britain, a more equitable Britain, but a land that remained British. The common people, seeing the success of industrial planning during the war, would welcome such economic strategies in peacetime—if the socialists could put their case well enough during the war.

Orwell liked his vision of Britain: he was creating a world in which he would enjoy living, a socialist state where he could still be George Orwell, free to write. But the real Britain of late 1940 could not be forgotten as he built his little book. The Germans were busy trying to destroy London. Orwell and Eileen could only rarely get out of London and to The Stores. Orwell missed his garden. London during the blitz (as the German bombardment was known) was a place of shortages, of blackouts, of sudden siren shrieks announcing the arrival of another flight of German bombers, the wait for the solid blast of the bombs that often fell nearby. But it was also a unified city, evidence in fact of the conclusions in Orwell's pamphlet. As 1941 neared the blitz intensified, but so did British effort and unity. Siege by air was accepted as a fact of life: Orwell could step calmly into a doorway to avoid an explosion's debris, then step calmly out and continue on his way. In bed at night he and Eileen could hear windows shatter. Orwell grew increasingly annoyed at his inability to win a job more actively involved in the war effort. He was as determined in early 1941 to serve his country as his father had been during World War I. The home guard was not enough: Orwell wanted to make a greater contribution.

His opportunity did not arrive until mid-August 1941, when he was asked to work for the British Broadcasting Corporation (BBC). Orwell would be responsible for writing and producing a variety of literary and cultural programs for BBC radio transmission to India and the Far East. Orwell joined the BBC propaganda machine somewhat warily: he had no interest in working on programs that presented the war as an effort to preserve capitalism or other aspects of a society he thought unjust and outmoded. But his objections were overcome by his subject matter. He broadcast discussions of poetry or dramatizations of short stories to intellectual audiences halfway around the globe. This activity neither preserved capitalism nor worked for socialism; it simply filled time, by the BBC's lights, and was not truly propaganda at all. Orwell found some humor in his situation, though he was still eager to become more directly involved in the war, even as he interviewed poet T. S. Eliot on the air or wrote the scripts of news broadcasts that he turned over to Indian announcers. He did not fit in well at the BBC, where virtually every word written had to be scrutinized by the Ministry of Information lest any words slip through that would displease the government. Worse than words were ideas, and scripts were occasionally censored or rejected because of their tone. Orwell understood the Ministry's demands and refused to bend to them. When he was asked to broadcast a new program himself, over the increasingly recognized Orwell name, he insisted that he be allowed to make clear his opposition to the government, though he restricted himself to news during his broadcasts. The microphone was emblazoned with the initials BBC, but Orwell took no official line.

He was doing a great deal of journalism as well, often writing at home late into the night after a full day at the BBC. Orwell and Eileen shared stories of the folly of censorship, of the machinations of bureaucracy, of the ease with which the truth could become lost as the government endeavored to manipulate public response. In his journalistic pieces Orwell felt more free to write of the revolution he perceived as beginning to take place in Britain. He undertook a regular letter of comment for the American left-wing journal, *Partisan Review*. He wrote other pamphlets and continued to review books. His BBC income allowed him to abandon the hack film and theater reviewing that he loathed and to concentrate on longer pieces. At the BBC he adapted stories by H. G. Wells and the Italian writer Ignazio Silone, but his own fiction was neglected. Orwell was also finding more prestigious markets open to him. His pieces began appearing in important journals and newspapers such as *The Tribune* and *The Observer*. *The Observer* became a particularly receptive home for his work, unafraid of Orwell's idiosyncracies or the habit he had of telling the truth as he saw it, and by so doing shocking the public.

Like many Londoners during the blitz, Orwell and Eileen found themselves changing lodgings occasionally when their apartment was damaged by bombs. Eileen left censorship for a job in the Ministry of Food, where she worked on radio broadcasts dealing with nutrition and cooking. Their increasingly infrequent visits to The Stores reminded them of the war's cost, and they both anticipated the end of the conflict when they could return to their garden full time and get back to serious work. Orwell put in his hours behind the typewriter and behind the microphone, but his frustration over the silliness, or at least the questionable value of his particular piece of the war effort grew. The British drove back Hitler's air power, the worst of the blitz receded, and tens of thousands of Americans began to arrive as the Allies prepared for the invasion of Europe. The preparations would take years. The long, gray middle of the war was around him, and by September 1943 Orwell had had enough. He resigned from the BBC.

By the end of the year he had become literary editor of *The Tribune*, and agreed to do a regular column for them. The column was called "As I Please," and its title described its subject matter. Orwell wrote of whatever caught his attention or struck his fancy; some of the columns were whimsical, others funny, others political. It was less a column of thought and idea, however, than of attitude and observation. Most of the columns

143

appeared as they were written directly on the typewriter: he rarely took notes or outlined these pieces. Orwell relaxed even more the informal style that made his long essays so readable, and he now wrote almost conversationally. "As I Please" could be counted upon to entertain and provoke, a personal column by a private man.

He had found simultaneously a form for his political thought. Orwell had never been satisfied with the political nature of his novels. He wanted to write fiction that told a gripping story but that also had something to say, and said it in a way that any reader could understand. His adaptations of stories at the BBC had sent him again and again through the mechanics of storytelling—pace, character, structure—while the pressures upon his time prevented him from undertaking the long novel he had for so long planned. Something shorter was called for, a return to serious writing, and after leaving the BBC Orwell began toying with an idea for a parable, almost a political fairy tale. He missed The Stores and the animals to whom he and Eileen always assigned names and attributed personalities. He worried about how the farm would do without his presence, even as he understood animals' superiority in some ways to humans. They were certainly stronger than humans, the larger animals, but they passed through life unaware of the power they possessed. Orwell began to write a story about a small English farm whose animals, aware at last of their own abilities, seize control and undertake the operation of the farm along their own lines.

Animal Farm was written quickly, despite Orwell's other commitments. He knew his setting, the farmyard; and he knew his characters, the pigs Napoleon and Snowball, the horses Boxer and Clover, the cows, dogs, chickens, sheep, and other animals whose masses rose to take control of their collective destiny. Such a story, however complex its underlying ideas and truths, must be told in only the simplest, most transparent prose, and Orwell made his as clear as a pane of glass. Eileen played a vital part in the creation of the new book. She had always made up stories about animals, and now she helped her husband plan out his own. She loved the story from the moment it was begun, but she also teased Orwell about the reception the book would receive. She predicted that critics and intellectuals, unable to see beyond their own interests and concerns, would take the book as evidence of Orwell's Trotskyite tendencies. For *Animal Farm* told the story of a revolution gone sour, losing itself in grandiose plans and ambitions at the expense of the individual. They would find Stalin's portrait in Napoleon, the boar whose power constantly increased, and they would take Orwell apart for his story of Snowball, who after much effort and sacrifice falls from official favor on the farm. Napoleon reveals that Snowball is not the revolutionary patriot his fellow animals believed him to be. He is a traitor, he has worked for the humans. Executions ensue on an order equal to any slaughter the animals had suffered under the old system. The revolution becomes complete.

Orwell was writing of larger themes than the rise of Stalin. One of the reasons he had selected his fantastic approach was that fantasy lifted *Animal Farm* above mere polemic. The book was universal, not topical.

The writing showed Orwell at his best. His simple sentences and dialogue allowed him to make political points a child could understand. And the book got off to a quick start, as Major, the oldest of the pigs, addressed the assembled animals, seeking to establish the rights of animals:

"'Comrades,' he said, 'here is a point that must be settled. The wild creatures, such as rats and rabbits—are they our friends or our enemies? Let us put it to the vote. I propose this question to the meeting: are rats comrades?'

"The vote was taken at once, and it was agreed by an overwhelming majority that rats were comrades. There were only four dissentients, the three dogs and the cat, who was afterwards discovered to have voted on both sides."

In addition to possessing great political truths and insights, *Animal Farm* was a very funny book. Orwell could make people chuckle even as they read his bitter view of politics and the corruption it fosters.

No matter how clever the book was—much less that it was a great book—*Animal Farm* would have trouble finding a publisher. Eileen's predictions proved accurate. Orwell was calm. When the manuscript was ready for submission in early March 1944, he wrote a letter to Gollancz predicting the publisher's unwillingness to accept the book. Gollancz was offended by Orwell's presumption, but read the manuscript and agreed that Orwell was correct. Secker and Warburg, Orwell knew, would take the book, but he also knew that he had written something more than a contemporary political piece: *Animal Farm* possessed universal appeal as a work of literature and he wanted, if possible, for the book to be backed by a major publisher. He sent the manuscript to Jonathan Cape, who took it to the Ministry of Information for an opinion. Orwell could have predicted their response as well: complaints that the book mocked the brave Soviet allies, disapproval of the intemperateness of tone, even a suggestion that an animal less offensive than the pig be chosen for the central characters. Orwell made his response in an "As I Please" *Tribune* piece about publishers, writing that "Circus dogs jump when the trainer cracks his whip, but the really well-trained dog is the one that turns his somersault when there is no whip."

His use of an animal as his metaphor was as deliberate as his choice of pigs for protagonists. The allusion, however, would be missed if he could not find a publisher. T. S. Eliot, rejecting the book for Faber and Faber, compared Orwell to Swift and made clear his recognition that Orwell had created a literary masterpiece. On the other hand, Faber could not publish the book because they did not agree with its political sympathies and sentiments. The rejections continued and Orwell began to consider publishing the book himself, even if it meant borrowing the money. By summer he had abandoned that idea and took the now ragged manuscript to Fred Warburg, who accepted it. The forthcoming contract that Warburg promised, however, met with many inexplicable delays.

Even as *Animal Farm* was being rejected, Orwell was making notes for a new novel. He would write a long book this time, one that would require careful planning and consideration. The effectiveness of his allegory encouraged him to try another form of fiction, the novel of a future, not of prediction but possibility. He called the book *The Last Man in Europe* and began building its dreary totalitarian world of permanent war, in which language, morality, and even thought are all subjugated to the control of the state. Orwell made notes and outlines.

Animal Farm was scheduled for publication in the summer of 1945—the longest wait Orwell had ever experienced for a book. Throughout the long wait he and Eileen enjoyed a most wonderful distraction. Despite the bombs bursting around them, they decided to adopt a son. As always, they were short of money, but Orwell and Eileen wanted to make their marriage complete. The child was brought to them in June 1944. They named the boy Richard Blair, after Orwell's father, and Richard's cries and coos mingled with the whine of the latest Nazi attempt to destroy London: V2 rocket bombs. Richard Blair, like his parents, accepted the presence of the war, a healthy, happy wartime child who became the center of his parents' lives. They made plans. The Stores would be too small for a family. Orwell looked for a new location, a farmhouse and a bit of land, the more remote the better. Richard arrived the month the invasion of Europe was at last launched, and the war would be over within a year. Orwell was eager to isolate himself, return to the raising of animals, get down to his next book.

Before the last shot was fired, though, Orwell wanted to see the front. By March 1945 he had maneuvered his way around the medical restrictions and had won himself a position as a war correspondent. He set off for France, eager for new experience.

He wrote several stories about the chaos he found in Europe, but the exertions of his trip exhausted him and his health collapsed. He thought that he would die, and composed a will with instructions regarding his literary estate, and mailed it to Eileen. He was not to hear from his wife again, though, for she was ill herself. Eileen died during what was supposed to be a routine gynecological operation on March 29, 1945. The news reached Orwell who, against the advice of physicians, left the French hospital and returned to London. He missed his wife's funeral. Weak, coughing, greatly depressed, he went from friend to friend, sometimes weeping, more often telling the story so matter-of-factly as to seem heartless. Orwell was lost.

He returned to Europe once his health was recovered and spent some time as a journalist. He did not linger long, for Richard needed him. The war against the Germans ended and publication, at last, of *Animal Farm* loomed, although the book had as yet found no American publisher willing to accept Orwell's fable. His sister Avril aided him in caring for Richard. Avril had moved to London with their mother early in the war, and both had worked for the war effort. But Ida Blair had died of a heart attack in 1943, and with Marjorie married and elsewhere, Avril felt as alone as her brother. Orwell looked for a permanent housekeeper and nanny, but also took to proposing to many of the women he met, some of them before knowing them a day. He could care for Richard himself, and he was a good and attentive father, but he wanted someone with whom to share his life. He told more than one of the women he met that it would not be a long life and his widow would have a healthy literary estate for her security.

It was odd, after all the years of small commissions and advances, to be able to make such a promise. After all the delays Warburg printed fewer than 5,000 copies of the book, but almost immediately ordered a second printing of 10,000. There remained no American publisher, but as the book's sales mounted there seemed little doubt that eventually there would be one.

The critical debate that Warburg had wanted for *Homage to Catalonia* erupted over *Animal Farm* and would not desist. Communist sympathizers resented the portrait of the noble ally that the Soviet Union, thanks to wartime propaganda, had become for much of the left. The far right, unexpectedly or at least ironically, adopted the book as a strictly anti-Stalin tract, and praised it. Some saw it as the story of Trotsky. All recognized that the book was magnificently written, and more than a few critics, even then, saw that *Animal Farm* was about far more than just one specific ruined revolution. Orwell, some recognized, as had T. S. Eliot, had attained the level of Jonathan Swift, whose *Gulliver's Travels* was praised and damned in its day for its narrow political interests, but can still be read because its truths are universal.

Orwell's income gave promise of rising dramatically as a result of the little book's success, and at last he seemed to come out of his despair over Eileen's death, at least somewhat. Not long after *Animal Farm* was published he hired Susan Watson, a woman of twenty-five with a child of her own, to care for Richard. He paid Susan well, and Richard responded to her affection and care. For herself Susan Watson quickly adjusted to the peculiarities of keeping house for George Orwell, the rest of the house falling to sleep to the tune of his typewriter as Orwell wrote through the night. He wrote through the days as well, occasionally going out or entertaining, but more often spending his waking time at his machine. The reputation Orwell had earned for being prolific was greatly enhanced in 1945 and 1946, as dozens of reviews and articles flooded from his typewriter. But they were all brief pieces, and though many of them were excellent, some of them masterpieces, none of them was more ambitious in scope than his wartime work. He continued to make notes for his novel, but postponed beginning it. *Animal Farm* was at last published in America by Harcourt Brace and was made a selection of the Book-of-the-Month Club. Orwell was famous.

He remained a private man and in 1946 began preparations to move himself, Richard, and Susan Watson out of London. He'd located a farm on the island of Jura, off the west coast of Scotland, that appealed to him. The farm was at the end of a seven-mile dirt road that connected it to its closest neighbor. The entire island had fewer than three hundred inhabitants and could be reached only by ferry. There was a single church, a single doctor, and a single town, Craighouse, at the opposite end of the island from Orwell's farm. He could not find a place more private in which to attempt a major work.

NINE

NINETEEN FORTY-EIGHT

ORWELL'S LEASED FARM WAS called Barnhill, and he made plans to visit it in May 1946. He was in the midst of a respite from work, having finally begun turning down journalistic assignments in an attempt to gather strength for the large novel that lay ahead. Orwell delayed his trip, sadly, to attend his sister Marjorie's funeral: she died of kidney disease at age forty-eight. Another link with Eric Blair's past was gone.

In late May he arrived at Barnhill alone, planning to ready it for summer occupancy by the entire family. Orwell responded favorably to the windswept rocks of Jura: it was a bleak place, but the temperature was far more kindly than that of many of the other Hebridean islands off the west coast of Scotland. Orwell planned to raise cattle, but Jura was not a suitable place; its soil was too acid to raise grain for stock that grazed on more than heather and grass. Barnhill itself was built of stone, and though not a large house had four bedrooms on its second floor. Orwell established a writing room for himself and worked to make the house comfortable. Avril joined him in late May, and by July Richard Blair and Susan Watson had made the journey from London to Jura. Susan did not stay long: the island's isolation may have played a part, and with Avril present there was tension as to who actually managed Orwell's home. Susan left before summer was out, after working for Orwell more than a year.

Throughout the summer Orwell gathered his strength but made no major effort on the new novel. He'd brought out another volume of critical essays, called just that, *Critical Essays*, early in 1946. On Jura he wrote more essays and reviews, but managed only a few thousand words of fiction. In *Animal Farm* he had taken a complex subject and treated it simply, which might be an apt definition of the fable form. Now, though, he wanted to create an entire, self-contained future world, not a prophecy, not a world of *the* future, but *a* future. It had to be believable and logical, for all of the exaggerations that would go into its making. Every element of the book and the world must work together to create a totally real portrait of a totalitarian world. He wanted on paper a reality the reader might feel as well as read. In October he, Avril, and Richard returned to London for the winter.

Orwell found living in a city as disagreeable as ever, and he was eager for winter to pass so that he could return to his island. His first season there had proved less productive than he had hoped, but it had also been a time of growing acquainted with his new home. On Jura he had been surrounded by openness, hills, and valleys; in London he was surrounded by squat drab buildings and advertising posters. He found the postwar world one of shortages more intense than those of the war years. The Labour Party had come into power at last, quite soon after the end of the war. But the revolution that Orwell had encouraged failed to follow suit. The Labour government in Orwell's view merely reinforced all that was bad about Britain, while abandoning any visionary alterations in the nation's or the government's nature. They were simply capitalists, the same old order, traveling under a Labour banner. To all the other fears of totalitarianism was now added the fear of nuclear destruction. Everything seemed uncertain, everyone, despite victory, somehow unfulfilled.

Early in 1947 Orwell made a solitary trip to Jura where he began an orchard. By April he was back on Jura with Avril and

Richard. His novel began to grow more rapidly, his stints at the typewriter grew longer and longer as he found his way through the story and his world. The previous winter had not been kind to his constitution, and it was nearly June before he was able to spend much time outdoors. Even as his health improved with the arrival of summer weather, Orwell stayed inside, working on the new book. He planned to complete the first draft by late summer or early fall, and limited the number of interruptions, journalistic or otherwise, that he allowed himself. He did take the time to write another long autobiographical essay, this one called "Such, Such Were the Joys," which contained in horrifying detail and almost savage prose his recollections of St. Cyprian's and the education it had afforded him.

Jura's remoteness did not dissuade occasional visitors from London's literary community. Perhaps more welcome were visitors from Orwell's family. Eileen's sister brought her own children for a long visit with Orwell. Marjorie's daughters came to visit their uncle, and he took their arrival as an opportunity to break off work on the new book and plan an adventure. He took them in a small boat to a remote spot for camping, where they could pretend to survive by their wits as had the boys in *The Coral Island.* Such survival became real on the return trip, when their boat's engine failed and they were stranded on a large rock until rescued by passing fishermen. Orwell enjoyed the experience tremendously. He became less willing even to consider returning to London; Jura was his home and he wanted to stay there year round.

Late in October he completed the draft of his novel. He had quite a job of revision ahead of him, but he was not up to it. The long hours of concentration had crushed his strength as completely as any illness, and by December he found himself committed once more to a sanatorium. He greeted New Year 1948 from a bed at Hairmyres Hospital, near Glasgow, Scotland. He might have to leave Jura but he would stay as close as he could. Orwell felt confined, shut in. Little things became important: he went to some trouble to obtain a ballpoint pen, a new invention at the time. There was no question of his being allowed a typewriter in the sanatorium. He endured several painful treatments intended to help his poor lungs heal. For six months he was unable to see his son. He wrote occasional articles and made notes for the revision of his novel. He anticipated his own death. Orwell was not released from Hairmyres until July and then he immediately returned to Jura, marshaling his strength by spending only half of each day on his feet, but learning quickly that he could work at his novel while in bed. The condition of his lungs grew worse.

Both *A Clergyman's Daughter* and *Keep the Aspidistra Flying* had opened with the chiming of clocks, and the new novel, as yet untitled, did as well. But Orwell wanted to establish from the first sentence of this new book that the world of which he wrote was not his own.

"It was a bright cold day in April and the clocks were striking thirteen," went the book's first sentence. By the second paragraph Orwell had begun establishing the particulars of his strange new world. "The hallway smelt of boiled cabbage and old rag mats. At one end of it a colored poster, too large for indoor display, had been tacked to the wall. It depicted simply an enormous face, more than a meter wide: the face of a man of about forty-five, with a heavy black mustache and ruggedly handsome features. Winston made for the stairs. It was no use trying the lift. Even at the best of times it was seldom working, and at present the electric current was cut off during daylight hours. It was part of the economy drive in preparation for Hate Week. The flat was seven flights up. . . . On each landing, opposite the lift shaft, the poster with the enormous face gazed down from the wall. It was one of those pictures which are so contrived that the eyes follow you about when you move. BIG BROTHER IS WATCHING YOU, the caption beneath it ran."

Orwell had spoken many times of his desire to try his hand at a ghost story, and the new novel, though its only ghosts were the ghosts of a half-remembered, better past, proved the most horrifying of his career. He transmuted the jackbooted boot crushing the human face into the story of Winston Smith, employee of the Ministry of Truth. It was one of the huge buildings that dominated the novel's London, and from which the nature of the world was defined for the people. It was a world of slogans such as FREEDOM IS SLAVERY and WAR IS PEACE. Government was managed by four Ministries, "the Ministry of Truth, which concerned itself with news, entertainment, education, and the fine arts; the Ministry of Peace, which concerned itself with war; the Ministry of Love, which maintained law and order; and the Ministry of Plenty, which was responsible for economic affairs." Britain was no longer called Britain, but Airstrip One, part of Oceania, one of the three great world powers.

Those powers waged constant war among each other, allegiances and alliances shifting with the winds of political expediency. Winston Smith and the other citizens of Oceania lived in a time of constant shortages, where there was little food, but plenty of telescreens to go around. The telescreens hung on the walls of the small filthy apartments, the medium through which Big Brother kept his citizens under observation. A new language, Newspeak, had been devised by the government; dissent, illegal anyway, was made impossible by the semantic rules of Newspeak. The government had created a language in which only encouragement for the government and its goals could be voiced. Thought police enforced those semantic rules, extending them from spoken and written language to thought itself. Winston Smith violates the law by keeping a diary and compounds his crime by falling in love. But the heart of Orwell's story was that Big Brother was watching.

Throughout the summer of 1948 he worked at the novel. If he recalled Eileen's teasing about the reception of *Animal Farm*, he may have considered the welcome his new novel was likely to earn. He did not want the book interpreted as a prediction, yet built into it were many elements satirizing his own experiences with the British Broadcasting Corporation (BBC) during the war. The novel's Ministry of Truth was located in a building clearly based upon the BBC's Broadcasting House. But, as with his farmyard allegory, he was also seeking to create a universal story, and in Winston Smith's desire for freedom of choice, freedom of expression, and freedom to love he touched universal concerns. Winston Smith's conflict with Big Brother gave the book a strong story. The government's manipulation of Smith's deepest fears gave the book a horrific heart. An essay on Newspeak, ostensibly historical, showed how language could be manipulated; the essay appeared as the afterword to Orwell's novel.

Orwell completed the final draft in late fall, but lacked the strength to take on the task of typing a clean manuscript. He tried to find a typist willing to come to Jura, but was finally forced to type it himself, ruining his precarious health with the effort. By January he was in the Cranham Sanatorium in England. But he had completed his novel and sent it to Secker and Warburg with the title he had last selected: *Nineteen Eighty-Four.*

The book promised to be an even larger success than *Animal Farm.* American publishers were now eager for Orwell's work, and the Book-of-the-Month Club offered £40,000 for the rights to the new novel, provided Orwell would make some alterations. He refused to change a word, and the Club took the book as it was. Orwell was not only famous, he was wealthy.

Cranham, the sanatorium to which he was confined, gave some evidence of his improved finances. He was given a small chalet of his own, well-heated and comfortable, surrounded by other chalets. Cranham lay high above sea level, and was a favored sanatorium of the upper classes. Orwell found himself surrounded by the types of people he disliked. It was easy for him to ignore them, though, for he spent most of his time in his quarters, and the physicians informed him that he might be confined to a bed for the rest of his life. He spoke of a new novel, and even wrote some reviews, but they took their toll. Whatever the results of his recuperation, his prolific days had ended with his collapse.

Orwell did receive a good amount of mail and was able, by violating doctors' orders, to answer much of it. A good deal of the correspondence contained wishes of improved health, and some of the letters touched Orwell deeply. One was from Jacintha Buddicom, his childhood friend and the first girl he had courted. She had read Orwell's work, but without any idea that he was Eric Blair until happening across a literary comment to that effect. She was a poet herself, and had evidently not married. Orwell wasted no time in his response, recounting his experiences since they'd last seen each other and writing a second letter with the Hail and Fare Well salutation they had used as children. His letter was handwritten because he was too weak to repair a minor problem with his typewriter. His loneliness showed through his words as he told his old friend of his child, and asked if she liked children. He invited Jacintha to visit him upon the return to London that he hoped would come soon.

Jacintha never visited, but Sonia Brownell did. She was a young woman, an editor, and Orwell had known her since shortly after Eileen's death. Their relationship had not been romantic, although Orwell proposed marriage to her. By the summer of 1949, as *Nineteen Eighty-Four* was published, he was working up his courage to propose again. He wanted to leave someone in charge of his estate and his son, should he die. The success of *Nineteen Eighty-Four*—its British first edition alone, which sold out quickly, was more than 25,000 copies—would make that estate sizable. *Animal Farm* was appearing throughout the world. The critics misunderstood Orwell, as always. Many of them saw the new novel as a renunciation of socialism. But once again many critics declared that Orwell was the equal of Swift. And a few wise reviewers, as always, saw that Orwell was not writing solely of temporal policies or politics, despite his transposition of the present year's numerals into his title. This time Orwell was too ill to respond other than perfunctorily to his critics. He made clear in a public statement that his book was no narrow satire of British socialism, but something larger; the statement, though, was issued in a paragraph rather than an essay. Orwell sank back into his bed.

On October 13, 1949, Orwell and Sonia Brownell were married. Orwell had been transferred to University College Hospital in London a month earlier. At forty-six he was fifteen years older than his new wife, and was unable to join the small wedding party at lunch after the ceremony. Everyone autographed the menu for the missing groom. A few days later he made a new will that provided for Richard and left the bulk of his estate to Sonia, putting her in charge of its management. His doctors recommended that he be moved to a sanatorium in Switzerland where the chill high air would be good for his lungs. Orwell tried to conserve his energy for the trip; he worried that he would be unable to get a proper cup of tea there. A. S. F. Gow, his old Eton tutor, came to visit, but gruffly announced that he was in the hospital to see someone else. Orwell shared a last afternoon with his son, and charged Avril, now married, with Richard's upbringing.

The New Year passed and Orwell made himself ready for the move to Switzerland. His optimism would not leave him, and he ordered a fishing rod packed with his belongings. After a few months in Switzerland he would be strong enough to fish a bit, and a few months after that he would be able to write once more. He wanted to be settled in before the end of the month.

Instead, on January 21, 1950, during the night, Orwell's lungs gave out in a final hemorrhage and he died quietly. The BBC paid tribute to him worldwide, and he was buried shortly afterward under a simple marker that read Eric Arthur Blair.

EPILOGUE

NINETEEN EIGHTY-FOUR IN 1984 (AND BEYOND)

ORWELL'S TELESCREENS LOOKED OUT on a world and its inhabitants, witnesses to every act in *Nineteen Eighty-Four*. In our own 1980s, we gaze into our television sets and are through their medium made witnesses to our own real world, and to the acts of its citizens and governments. In many ways, our situation seems the opposite of the world envisioned by George Orwell. And why not: despite the opinions offered by many critics, and the beliefs of a great number of readers, Orwell did not intend his novel as prophecy, certainly not as technological prophecy, or even as strict speculation about the future. *Nineteen Eighty-Four* is a story, a novel with characters and plot, that takes place in a world fashioned from some of the materials of our own world, but also from pieces of Orwell's imagination.

Yet the novel possesses a tremendous realistic charge: as we read we are convinced absolutely of that world's existence, it becomes more real with each page turned, and stays with the reader after the book is closed and laid aside. George Orwell, coughing at his typewriter, achieved *Nineteen Eighty-Four*'s great power through the accretion of telling details, through the universality of the fears that serve as the book's fulcrum, through his own mastery of the English language, as well as his masterful creation, Newspeak. The novel's power is such that for many readers and indeed for many who have never opened the book, this novel published in 1949 served as a portrait, painted in advance and fixed forever, of 1984.

The novel entered and affected language and thought as few other books have done. Big Brother became a synonym for governmental power, and lately for corporate power. Big Brother's name, and his ceaseless watching, have been invoked by pundits and public alike since the novel was first published. Orwell struck a chord, or a nerve, creating an archetype that will probably stand forever, two words capable of conjuring an image of awesome, awful control. It is not only the state's power that Orwell warns of in *Nineteen Eighty-Four;* it is the use of that power for the control of its subjects, their thoughts, and their language. For more than three decades, now, every example of increased governmental power, or decreased individual freedom, has been labeled in democratic states, as well as totalitarian ones, as one more example of Big Brother's rise, or his imminent arrival.

Evidence of Newspeak can be heard and seen throughout our world as well. Language, human beings' most magnificent creation, remains one of the great weapons, or tools, employed by governments to justify or hide their actions. We can see examples of this daily, as totalitarian states announce over the sound and smoke of invasion that they and their troops had simply responded to invitations, entering nations as guests, their weapons the sort of gift any good guest brings. More than one dissident has been placed in "protective custody," incarceration intended to protect the dissident from his or her own ideas and attitudes. The name of the Russian newspaper *Pravda* means "Truth."

But democracies are also susceptible to this sort of abuse of language to disguise their acts or distract their citizens. The United States has fought more than one war by "invitation" and labeled it a "police action," or identified "invasions" as "rescues."

Britain sent a fleet to sail over eight thousand miles, almost halfway around the world, in order to engage in a "defensive action" in the Falkland Islands.

In *Nineteen Eighty-Four* the world engaged in constant small wars, as an economic and political necessity. Without wars, the economy would collapse. But with wars grown too large—or employing nuclear weapons—the stability of the state would be destroyed. So, in Orwell's novel, war becomes one more product, its nature regulated and controlled, an aspect of life that is unceasing and that cannot be questioned. As the slogan in the novel goes, WAR IS PEACE.

1984's military machine grinds on as well. The manufacture of conventional weapons and their use in "small" wars mounts. An economy can be made to boom when the spark of increased defense spending is struck. The point is made throughout the world, however, that the expense is for *defense,* not war.

In Orwell's world an accommodation had been made with the existence of nuclear weapons. In our own world, we begin as children to make a psychological adjustment to those weapons' existence. Thermonuclear bombs, capable of eradicating all life from the face of the planet, continue to be produced, their existence justified because they are required for the maintenance of peace. More nuclear bombs are needed in order to maintain more peace. Nuclear war cannot come, governments announce, so long as the assurance of destruction is shared by the adversaries. *Mutually assured destruction* is intended as a comforting phrase. Language thus used soon ceases to have any real meaning: it becomes one more tool of control.

The computer, so central to every aspect of our 1984, has it both ways: it serves as a ferocious generator of vague language and jargon, and it is also seen by many as Big Brother incarnate. We each of us are coded and encoded, the particulars of our lives, our education, our financial histories, our relations with the police, for some people their very opinions—all are stored in vast memory banks, accessible to the government and other institutions, places from which we may be watched. Big Brother's face, if we accept him metaphorically as the computer, may well be the cathode ray tube, that television monitor on which, digitally, our lives may be played and replayed in search of condemnatory evidence, or grounds for accusation or reward, or whatever combination of information is sought. Legal systems worldwide struggle to come to terms with the ways in which the computer is changing the fabric of society. The right to privacy, so essential to freedom, seems to shrink daily. Like Winston Smith in Orwell's novel, many have come to seek a position from which they cannot be watched. Such positions are no longer easy to find: even hermits must have social security numbers.

The computer's tendrils reach as well to the heart of language, creating new words and arrangements of words, subsuming old words and rendering them inappropriate in reference to anything but computers, fabricating an entire language of their own. Our store of knowledge is no longer a living thing, a *body;* it has become a *database.* Nouns become verbs, as in *access,* as in the government's ability to access our records and thereby our lives. Machine language drives human language into unfamiliar and sometimes tortuous constructions. Software is required to operate hardware, and together, many feel, they conspire to run our lives. Scientists seek to fabricate artificial intelligence, and give the computer the powers of reason, intuition, imagination, and judgment, but many fear it is they who will be judged. Has Big Brother arrived?

He arrived, in the most important sense, the moment George Orwell created him, and his presence has been felt from the moment Big Brother's name appeared in print. *Nineteen Eighty-Four* changed the way people think. Nowhere can that more clearly be seen than in the adoption of the author's name to describe the tendencies and trends that he so loathed: they are called *Orwellian.* The word, of course, did not exist during Eric Blair's lifetime, but it is likely that it will linger long after our own. Orwell's life and work served the cause of freedom, and there are few better ways to serve that cause then by labeling its adversaries. That is, and always shall be, an Orwellian boot stamping on freedom's face. No simpler, more striking portrait can be drawn of totalitarianism.

Our information age, then, is also an Orwellian age, and the arrival of 1984 fostered a flurry of commentary and consideration. The year that had loomed so large for so long was at last upon us.

Anticipation of it had been growing since 1949. The same questions existed then. Was Orwell's novel a work of prophecy, was this what lay ahead? Was it a satire, or a horror story? Did this future have to come about? Some critics have argued persuasively that Orwell wrote of 1948, deriving his title from the simple transposition of that year's terminal digits. The Ministry of Truth was simply the British Broadcasting Corporation (BBC); the despair and deprivations of *Nineteen Eighty-Four*'s world nothing less than a distorted reflection of Britain's postwar economy. *Nineteen Eighty-Four* was only 1948, made grotesque.

But the novel's title seems deliberate. It is not, after all, a date, but words, a description, *Nineteen Eighty-Four*, yet its proximity served to give every reader pause. The novel's first readers had only thirty-five years between themselves and 1984; and each day the book was in print brought the dread date closer. A sort of schizophrenia developed as the years passed: evidence could be found everywhere that Orwell was wrong about many of the particulars of the future, but equally there was also evidence that Orwell was wrong *only* in his particulars. The novel portrayed the future, but also defined it, anticipated it, but in many minds also helped create it. *Nineteen Eighty-Four* was read, taught, discussed, and studied, its influence growing with each year. *Animal Farm* was perhaps more often taught, but *Nineteen Eighty-Four* was the book of which everyone had heard.

Other books were written to explain it. The calendar year 1984 lay close enough to permit other writers and thinkers their own predictions and anticipations, more than a few of them cast to show how Orwell had erred in his own speculation.

Nigel Calder, one of Britain's most influential and effective science writers and editors, took advantage of 1964's two-decade gap to create an anticipatory anniversary, as it were. To focus upon 1984 minus twenty years, Calder invited a variety of scientists, writers, and other thinkers to contribute their own visions of 1984 to *The New Scientist,* a highly respected British science magazine. The predictions ranged far, through the hard and soft sciences, from technology to whimsy, from optimism (Orwell's world would not come to be) to pessimism (Orwell's world became more likely each day). The contributions were collected by Calder in a book called *The World in 1984.* In books of his own, and other collections that he edited, Nigel Calder continued through the sixties and seventies to anticipate the arrival of 1984, to examine Orwell's precepts and ideas, to seek congruencies between them and the real world.

Six years ahead of 1984's arrival, Anthony Burgess wrote a book called *1985.* Burgess, a brilliant and prolific British writer whose novels include *A Clockwork Orange* and *Earthly Powers,* divided *1985* into three parts. A long introductory dialogue allowed Burgess to recapitulate the essence of *Nineteen Eighty-Four,* with a series of brief essays following, in which he offered his criticisms of the novel both as prophecy and as a work of literature. The heart of the book, a novella called *1985,* permitted Burgess his own picture of the future, different from Orwell's, of course, depressing and grim, though not so terrifying as the world of *Nineteen Eighty-Four.* Burgess, whose linguistic playfulness and insight is a hallmark of his work, even invented his own language, Workers' English. An epilogue was used to draw the strands of his argument together. *1985* is what Burgess called a cacotopian novel—a portrait of a world in which the tendencies toward a utopia result in the creation of a grim, gray state.

But Orwell's novel was a dystopia, the opposite of a utopia, and his terrible vision would not leave people alone. Calder's books and Burgess's response were only two of a stream of publications that dealt with Orwell's work. By late 1983 the stream had become a torrent.

George Orwell, dead for more than three decades, appeared on the cover of the November 28, 1983 issue of *Time* magazine, and seven pages of the issue were devoted to examining Orwell's life, presenting excerpts from his work, reminding readers that 1984 was upon them. For a week, late in 1983, in pastel and charcoal, Orwell's face stared out from magazine covers.

Nigel Calder, never one to leave a job undone, revisited the twenty-year-old predictions from *The World in 1984* and other books, and enlisted literary assistance in their evaluation. His assistant was an imaginary computer named O'Brien, and a dialogue between Calder and O'Brien is the format chosen by Calder for a book entitled *1984 and Beyond* (called in Britain *1984 and After*). O'Brien, the reader learns quickly, is short for *Omniscient Being Re-Interpreting Every Notation*, but we are also aware that O'Brien was a major character in *Nineteen Eighty-Four*. By way of dialogue between himself and his supercomputer, Calder not only updates, corrects, and criticizes the predictions made in earlier years, he also examines the real world of 1984, and the likelihood of Orwell's vision becoming a reality.

By Christmas week, 1983, Orwell's name seemed on everyone's lips. A countdown to 1984 was begun. Sales of paperback copies of the novel—its title incorrectly printed in bright colored numerals, *1984*—began to mount. Those who had known Orwell, or Eric Blair, found themselves beset by journalists from around the world. Madame Tussaud's London wax museum added George Orwell, six-foot-three of sculpted wax, to its displays. Flowers were sent to the church where Orwell was buried. The last week of 1983 passed. New Year's Eve parties were held, some of them requiring revelers to attend in *Nineteen Eighty-Four*-esque costumes, gray and dingy; the dead author's health was drunk. One year ended and another arrived, but it was Orwell's New Year as well as the calendar's.

The New Year arrived on a Sunday, and agnostic Orwell's name served as the focus for sermons. Television sets on January 1, 1984, carried Orwell's seamed face, and commentators spoke, often incorrectly, of his career. A radio broadcast was begun of a seven-part oral biography of Orwell that included many reminiscences of Eric Blair by those who had known him. Sunday comic strips, including *Peanuts*, used Orwell or his book as their subject matter. His name was on the front page of many newspapers, and on the editorial and book pages of virtually all. That year was here.

The year would in fact be present for 366 days, but Orwell's name faded fast from the headlines. A profile appeared of him in *People* magazine, along with a sidebar telling of Richard Blair, Orwell's adopted son, 39 in 1984 and with a family of his own. At the end of the first week of January, *New Times*, a Soviet magazine, informed its readers that Orwell's vision had been made a reality in the United States, that Ronald Reagan was Big Brother, and even quoted from Orwell's book, which is banned in the Soviet Union. In the free world *Nineteen Eighty-Four*, always a steady seller, climbed to the top of most paperback bestseller lists.

By the end of January Orwell's name was appearing less frequently in print, although observations of his impact and celebrations of his life continued to take place. More books were published, some of them seeking new ways of approaching Orwell. *Orwell for Beginners* by David Smith and Michael Mosher used comic book art and calligraphy to illuminate Orwell's work. Bernard Crick's *George Orwell: A Life*, which had appeared in 1980 and been revised a year later, continued to attract readers, contributing greatly to the understanding of Orwell's life and the ways in which it related to his work. Crick himself embarked on a 1984 lecture tour of the United States, and spent time with both university and high-school students, sharing with them his sound insights into Orwell. Many colleges, universities, and high schools held special Orwell seminars or symposia. The Smithsonian Institution planned Orwell lectures; the Library of Congress scheduled a conference on Orwellian themes; new editions of Orwell's work appeared.

The Jura Hotel in Craighouse (Jura) undertook several "Special Weeks" during which tourists and guests would be treated to discussions of Orwell's life and work. A high point was to be a trip up the island to visit Barnhill, where *Nineteen Eighty-Four* took shape.

In the middle of 1984, after much of the furor over Orwell had passed, his name appeared again in headlines in a way that might have amused him. Approximately 250,000 previously unpublished words of Orwell's work were discovered in London. The work included a great many letters, but, more importantly, sixty-two of his radio scripts for the BBC. The scripts for the program "Through Eastern Eyes" had been missing since Orwell left the BBC during the war. They were discovered by William J. West, who was doing research in the BBC files. No previous search had unearthed the work because it was filed, not under Orwell's name, or even the name of his program, but under the name of the Indian announcers who had read the work over the air. It was the typical sort of bureaucratic blunder that Orwell had found so annoying and amusing. The works were published in book form before the end of 1984. Orwell's name soon vanished from the press once more.

The arrival of 1984, then, was an event, but one that was displaced by other events. In the United States 1984 was a presidential election year, and the political language of the campaign seemed to bear Orwellian fruit: whole weeks were occupied with arguments over how things were said, rather than debates over what was being said.

Internationally, the public debate over nuclear weapons grew more heated, even as discussions between the United States and the Soviet Union over the regulation and reduction of those weapons broke down. A new element entered the arena, as the use of outer space as a strategic location for "defensive weapons" became a topic of angry discussion. This was 1984, after all, and to negotiators and opposing governments, defensive weapons were really offensive ones, and thus could not be allowed. Andrei Sakharov, the great Russian physicist and dissident, disappeared; rumors circulated midyear that he was undergoing various types of brainwashing to make him better "understand" the Soviet government.

The debate over *Nineteen Eighty-Four* continued in magazines and books, if not in the daily press. Democratic governments used the novel as a portrait of totalitarian ones, just as the Soviet Union presented the novel as a clear picture of the United States. Nor did literary critics cease trying to determine if the novel were a satire, a novel, an allegory, or something unique unto itself. Bookstore clerks were asked for "that book of predictions," Orwell serving for many as a modern Nostradamus.

But George Orwell, coughing his lungs out on Jura, dying as he revised the work, was no prophet at all. He set himself a goal in *Nineteen Eighty-Four,* as in all of his work, of simply telling the truth as he saw and understood it. That he saw clearly is revealed in that very zeal with which various opposing camps seize Orwell and his work as support for their views. The story of Winston Smith has been interpreted as an attack on Soviet Communism, on British socialism, on capitalism, on fascism, on whatever "ism" is currently fashionable or unfashionable. The book has been used, narrowly, by ideologues right, left, and in the center as a bulwark for their beliefs about the world and its villains.

Nineteen Eighty-Four, though, is no narrow novel, and the size of its impact and its audience reveal that the book speaks clearly to all who read it, that it has something to say to everyone. The novel is as politically sound today as when it was published, and that soundness gives an indication that the book is above topical politics. How many times has the world changed since 1949? The world is changing even as this book is written, and will continue to change even as you read. Yet *Nineteen Eighty-Four* still speaks to us of dangers, still frightens us with what it shows, still moves us to be more wary in our endorsement of any political system or idea.

We live in a dangerous world. But Orwell's work reminds us that it is a world of our own making. Big Brother may wish to watch us, but in a free state we may also watch him. Language remains the people's possession, and free people have it within their power to refuse to take seriously the semantic games their leaders play, and to insist, by votes and dissent, that the leaders speak more clearly, more honestly, in better service of truth. The computer that stores information about us also gives us far greater powers. Through computers a vast body of knowledge and information is available to us, far more than has ever before been available to human beings. The computer, we should always be aware, is a machine, and its language is our own invention; artificial intelligence research may teach us more about the way we ourselves learn than we have ever before known.

Even nuclear weapons may be seen as among civilization's assets. No aspect of civilization has served so dramatically as a focus not simply for one political party or two, or one nation or two, but for all of the citizens of the world. The greatest ally a totalitarian government may have is the silence of the people. Nuclear weapons have rendered not only warfare, but also silence obsolete. The bombs possess the power to destroy civilization, but also to galvanize it, to bring together rather than to blow apart. The bookstores of 1984 were filled with copies of *Nineteen Eighty-Four*, the streets were filled with people saying *enough*.

Our endeavor to avoid the world of *Nineteen Eighty-Four* must not end simply because 1984 passes. Winston Smith dates his diary entry 1984, but is not certain that the date is correct. The date does not matter: Orwell's novel is true for 1949, as well as 1984, and for all the years in between and afterward. What matters are Orwell's truths, which because he was a great writer, are also our truths. We have survived the arrival of 1984, but can never rest in our efforts to avoid and overcome those tendencies toward *Nineteen Eighty-Four* that are, perhaps inherently, a part of every government.

Orwell knew this and he wrote this. In free nations today his works are available, in the sort of "collected editions" that he had so longed for in his youth.

ACKNOWLEDGMENTS
AND REFERENCES

My friend Wayne Donnell of Greensboro, a literate man, provided important research materials at just the right moment in my preparations for this book, and I would like to begin my acknowledgments by thanking him.

My brother, Ed Ferrell, provided a base of operations and a source of good advice on research when I was in New York. Herb Katz of M. Evans, and Henry Morrison, formerly of Greenwich Village, both helped as I gathered some perspective on Orwell, as did Leslie Owen. Diane Gedymin saw to it that this book is so attractive.

Linda Cabasin of M. Evans proved once more her abilities as an editor. Her accessibility, insight, and sense of humor were as always invaluable.

Even more accessible were, and are, my wife Martha and my son Alec. They both heard more about George Orwell than they may have wished to hear, but I could not have written this book without them.

The major sources for this biography were these:

Bernard Crick's *George Orwell: A Life* (New York: Atlantic/ Little, Brown, 1980). Professor Crick's book is exhaustive but not exhausting, a major biographical effort that is a pleasure to read and rewarding to contemplate. The volume of material examined and documented is staggering. The book is effectively organized, with a valuable long introductory essay that establishes the author's attitude toward his subject and his sources, while at the same time offering provocative comment and reflection upon the nature of biography. Professor Crick's knowledge of Orwell and Orwell's work is equaled or surpassed by his understanding of political, social, and literary contexts. This is a fine close-up history of an era as well as an individual.

It was my pleasure to hear Bernard Crick speak as I was writing this book. His opinions are as sound and clear in person as on the page; so sound that when one disagrees with his conclusions, one is forced to think especially hard and carefully. Surely that is a sign of an important work, and an important writer. The last decade of Orwell's life was, of necessity, treated only briefly in the present book. It was, however, a rich and event-filled time in Orwell's life, to which fully a third of Professor Crick's book is devoted. Anyone who wishes to learn more about Orwell should turn immediately to *George Orwell: A Life*. Should the political context of that life appeal, Professor Crick's bibliography and a bibliography of Professor Crick's other distinguished works will serve well as guides.

Peter Stansky and William Abraham wrote a two-volume study of Orwell's life through the Spanish Civil War. *The Unknown Orwell* (New York: Alfred A. Knopf, 1972) carries Orwell through the publication of *Down and Out in Paris and London*. *Orwell: The Transformation* (New York: Alfred A. Knopf, 1980) follows Orwell through his escape from Spain. Although the authors perhaps accept too much of Orwell's own work as authoritative, their interpretation of his life and its psychological underpinnings is interesting. The books are clearly written and chronologically organized.

Jacintha Buddicom, Eric Blair's childhood friend, became a poet. Her reminiscence of their youth, *Eric and Us* (London: Leslie Frewin, 1974) is a poignant story that offers a gentle picture of the youth of Eric Blair and their friendship. While

172

Eric and Us is a personal, rather than a documented, biography, it should prove of interest to all who wish to know more about the Blair from whom Orwell grew.

As with the subject of any literary biography, the best place for readers to learn more about the subject is with his own works. Eric Blair dreamed of a collected edition of his works, and that edition is becoming available now.

THE WORKS OF GEORGE ORWELL

1933

Down and Out in Paris and London, Orwell's first book, his personal (fictionalized) account of poverty in France and England.

1934

Burmese Days, Orwell's first formal novel.

1935

A Clergyman's Daughter, Orwell's second novel, the most self-consciously experimental of his works.

1936

Keep the Aspidistra Flying, Orwell's third novel, the story of Gordon Comstock.

1937

The Road to Wigan Pier, Orwell's account of his trip to Britain's industrial heart, and his attack on socialism as practiced.

1938

Homage to Catalonia, Orwell's account of the Spanish Civil War, and the collapse of political idealism.

1939

Coming Up for Air, Orwell's fourth novel, the story of George Dowling.

174

1940

Inside the Whale, Orwell's first essay collection.

1940

The Lion and the Unicorn, the first of The Searchlight Books.

1945

Animal Farm, Orwell's political fable.

1946

Critical Essays (In America: *Dickens, Dali and Others*), Orwell's second collection of essays.

1949

Nineteen Eighty-Four, Orwell's final novel.

1950

Shooting an Elephant, a posthumous essay collection.

1953

Such, Such Were the Joys, a posthumous essay collection.

1953

England Your England, a posthumous essay collection.

1968

The Collected Essays, Journalism and Letters of George Orwell, a massive edition consisting of four thick volumes that incorporate material from Orwell's previous collections, uncollected essays and journalism, diaries and private papers, journalism and reviews, correspondence and miscellaneous items. Edited by Sonia Brownell Orwell and Ian Angus, this collection runs to 2,000 pages and displays Orwell's achievement in its contents, and his prolificity in its bulk. One obtains from these books a sense of how very hard and constantly Orwell worked. Each book is arranged carefully, with items documented and, where necessary, the context of correspondence explained. These four volumes are a priceless literary and biographical collection. In order, the volumes are:

I. *An Age Like This,* covering the years 1920–1940, with the 1946 essay "Why I Write" serving as a preface to the entire series.

II. *My Country Right or Left,* with selections from 1940–1943, including the complete text of *The Lion and the Unicorn.*

III. *As I Please,* covering the last years of World War II, 1943–1945 and including many of Orwell's "As I Please" columns.

IV. *In Front of Your Nose,* with material from the last years of Orwell's life, and including "Such, Such Were the Joys," his still controversial essay about St. Cyprian's.

INDEX

Act for the Better Government of India, 13

Adelphi, 91, 93, 106, 117

Animal Farm, 144–148, 152, 163

Blair, Avril (sister), 17, 32, 34, 148, 151, 152, 158

Blair, Charles (great-great grandfather), 9

Blair, Charles, Jr. (great grandfather), 9

Blair, Eileen (wife), 108, 109, 111, 112, 119, 120–121, 127, 128–129, 130, 131, 134, 135, 137, 142, 143, 144–145, 147, 148

Blair, Eric
born, 15
in Burma, 63–76
at Eton, 46–59
marries, 120–121, 158
in Paris, 83–89
pseudonym chosen, 95–96
at St. Cyprian's, 23–44
in Spain, 122–132
at Sunnylands school, 17–20
as teacher, 94–95, 103
at Wellington College, 45–46

Blair, Ida Limouzin (mother), 14–17, 20, 32, 37–38, 50, 52, 77–78, 89–90, 148

Blair, Marjorie (sister), 14, 16, 17, 18, 32, 34, 52, 117, 151

Blair, Richard (son), 147, 151, 152, 158, 166

Blair, Richard Walmsley (father), 11, 13–14, 16, 18, 21, 32, 50, 52, 77–78, 89–90, 136

Blair, Thomas Richard Arthur (grandfather), 9–11

Blitz (London), 141, 143

Book-of-the-Month Club, 156

Booklover's Corner, 106–107

British Broadcasting Corporation (BBC), 141–142, 143, 144, 156, 163

British Union of Fascists, 118

Brownell, Sonia, 157, 158

Buddicom, Jacintha, 35–36, 40, 55, 56, 58, 60, 66, 67, 157

Buddicom, Prosper, 35, 40, 55, 56, 60

Burgess, Anthony, 164, 165

Burma (history), 63–64

Burmese Days, 101–105, 106, 108, 109

Butler, Samuel, 72, 84

Calder, Nigel, 164, 165

"Censure en Angleterre," 85–86

Clergyman's Daughter, 106, 107–108, 154

Coming Up for Air, 136

Communists, 114, 124, 125, 126–

127, 128, 129–130, 131, 134, 137

Computers, 161–162, 169

Connolly, Cyril, 35, 110

Crick, Bernard, 166

Critical Essays, 152

Days in London and Paris (Down and Out in Paris and London), 94, 95

Dos Passos, John, 100

Down and Out in Paris and London, 96–99

East India Company, 12, 13

Eliot, T. S., 93, 94, 146

Erewhon, 72

Eton, 41, 46–59

Fabian Society, 114

Faulkner, William, 100

Frays College, 103

Gollancz, Victor, 95, 98, 104, 107–108, 110, 111, 112, 117, 122, 123–124, 130, 136, 138, 146

Gow, A. S. F., 48, 79, 158

Gulliver's Travels, 18, 149

"Hanging, A," 92–93

Hare, Francis, 11

Harper Brothers, 97, 105, 106

Hawthorns school, 94–95, 103

Heinemann, 104

Hemingway, Ernest, 100

Homage to Catalonia, 130, 131–132, 133–134, 135, 149

Home Guard, 139, 140

Huxley, Aldous, 71, 100

Independent Labour Party (ILP), 114, 121, 125, 126, 130, 134–135, 137

Insein, Burma, 72–73

Inside the Whale, 137–138

Jaques, Eleanor, 102

Joyce, James, 100–101, 106

Jura, 151–152, 153, 167

Keep the Aspidistra Flying, 111, 117, 119, 133, 154

King's Scholars (Eton), 41, 43, 45–46

Kipling, Rudyard, 72

Kitchener, Lord, 42

Last Man in Europe, 147

Lawrence, D. H., 100

Limouzin, Nellie, 83

Limouzin family, 74

Lion and the Unicorn, 140

London, Jack, 56–57

Mandalay, Burma, 63–64

Maugham, W. Somerset, 71–72

Miller, Henry, 122, 124

Mr. Britling Sees It Through, 54

Moore, Leonard, 99

Mosher, Michael, 166

Mosley, Oswald, 118

Myaungmya, Burma, 68

Myers, L. H., 135

National Unemployed Workers' Movement (NUWM), 114

New Adelphi. See Adelphi
New Scientist, 164
New Times, 166
Newspeak, 155, 160
1985, 164
Nineteen Eighty-Four, 153–156,
    157–158, 159–161, 162–170
1984 and Beyond, 165
Nuclear weapons, 161, 167–168,
    169

Obermeyer, Rosalind, 108, 111
Observer, The, 143
Officers' Training Corps (Eton),
    52–53
"On a Ruined Farm near the His
    Master's Voice Gramophone
    Factory," 106
Opium, 11–13
Orwell, George. *See* Blair, Eric
Orwell for Beginners, 166
O'Shaughnessy, Eileen. *See* Blair,
    Eileen (wife)

Pacifism, 52, 54
Partisan Review, 142
Patriotism, 139–140
People of the Abyss, 56
Pitter, Ruth, 79, 80
POUM (Partido Obrero de
    Unificacíon Marxista), 125–
    127, 128, 130, 134
Priestley, J. B., 98
Primogeniture, 9

Rangoon, Burma, 63–64
Road to Wigan Pier, 123–124,
    129–130

Sakharov, Andrei, 168
*Scullion's Diary (Down and Out in
    Paris and London)*, 90, 92
Secker and Warburg, 130, 133–
    134, 140, 146, 156
Sheffield, 116–117
Shiplake, 33–34, 35
"Shooting an Elephant," 120
Smith, David, 166
Socialism, 54, 122–123, 131, 139–
    141
Southwold, 90, 104, 105, 106, 136
Spain, 122–132, 134, 136
"Spike," 91
"Spilling the Spanish Beans," 129
St. Cyprian's, 20, 23–44
Stores (Wallington), 118–119, 121,
    124, 129, 130, 135, 136
"Such, Such Were the Joys," 153
Swift, Jonathan, 18, 149
Syriam, Burma, 71

Time, 165
Time and Tide, 138
Tribune, The, 143–144
Tropic of Cancer, 122, 138
Trotsky, Lev Davidovich, 125, 149
Twante, Burma, 68–70

Ulysses, 100–101
United Marxist Workers' Party.
    See POUM

Wallington, 118
Warburg, Fredric, 130, 147, 149
Watson, Susan, 149–150, 151
Wellington College, 41, 45–46

Wells, H. G., 37, 53–54
"Wells, Hitler, and the World
    State," 139
West, William J., 167
Wigan, 115–116
Wilkes, Vaughan, 20–21, 26–27,

28–29, 31, 32, 38, 41, 42, 43,
    44
Wilkes, Mrs. Vaughan, 20–21, 25,
    26–27, 31, 32, 38, 43
World in 1984, 164, 165
World War I, 37, 39–40, 51–52